Changing News Use

Changing News Use pulls from empirical research to introduce and describe how changing news user patterns and journalism practices have been mutually disruptive, exploring what journalists and the news media can learn from these changes.

Based on 15 years of audience research, the authors provide an in-depth description of what people do with news and how this has diversified over time, from reading, watching, and listening to a broader spectrum of user practices including checking, scrolling, tagging, and avoiding. By emphasizing people's own experience of journalism, this book also investigates what two prominent audience measurements – clicking and spending time – mean from a user perspective. The book outlines ways to overcome the dilemma of providing what people apparently want (attention-grabbing news features) and delivering what people apparently need (what journalists see as important information), suggesting alternative ways to investigate and become sensitive to the practices, preferences, and pleasures of audiences and discussing what these research findings might mean for everyday journalism practice.

The book is a valuable and timely resource for academics and researchers interested in the fields of journalism studies, sociology, digital media, and communication.

Irene Costera Meijer is Professor of Journalism Studies at Vrije Universiteit Amsterdam. She is a world-leading journalism and media scholar, having recently set the agenda for the audience turn in journalism studies. Her research has appeared in many journals and books and focuses on what news users value about journalism.

Tim Groot Kormelink is Assistant Professor of Journalism Studies at Vrije Universiteit Amsterdam. His work centers around capturing and making sense of everyday news use and has appeared in such journals as *Journalism, Journalism Studies, Digital Journalism, Media, Culture & Society*, and *International Journal of Press/Politics*.

Disruptions: Studies in Digital Journalism
Series editor: Bob Franklin

Disruptions refers to the radical changes provoked by the affordances of digital technologies that occur at a pace and on a scale that disrupts settled understandings and traditional ways of creating value, interacting and communicating both socially and professionally. The consequences for digital journalism involve far reaching changes to business models, professional practices, roles, ethics, products and even challenges to the accepted definitions and understandings of journalism. For Digital Journalism Studies, the field of academic inquiry which explores and examines digital journalism, disruption results in paradigmatic and tectonic shifts in scholarly concerns. It prompts reconsideration of research methods, theoretical analyses and responses (oppositional and consensual) to such changes, which have been described as being akin to 'a moment of mind-blowing uncertainty'.

Routledge's new book series, *Disruptions: Studies in Digital Journalism*, seeks to capture, examine and analyse these moments of exciting and explosive professional and scholarly innovation which characterize developments in the day-to-day practice of journalism in an age of digital media, and which are articulated in the newly emerging academic discipline of Digital Journalism Studies.

Smartphones and the News
Andrew Duffy

What is Digital Journalism Studies?
Steen Steensen and Oscar Westlund

Changing News Use
Unchanged News Experiences?
Irene Costera Meijer and Tim Groot Kormelink

For more information, please visit: www.routledge.com/Disruptions/book-series/DISRUPTDIGJOUR

Changing News Use

Unchanged News Experiences?

**Irene Costera Meijer and
Tim Groot Kormelink**

Routledge
Taylor & Francis Group

LONDON AND NEW YORK

First published 2021
by Routledge
2 Park Square, Milton Park, Abingdon, Oxon OX14 4RN

and by Routledge
52 Vanderbilt Avenue, New York, NY 10017

Routledge is an imprint of the Taylor & Francis Group, an informa business

British Library Cataloguing-in-Publication Data
A catalogue record for this book is available from the British Library

Library of Congress Cataloging-in-Publication Data
A catalog record for this book has been requested

ISBN: 978-0-367-48578-8 (hbk)
ISBN: 978-1-003-04171-9 (ebk)

Typeset in Times New Roman
by Apex CoVantage, LLC

Contents

Acknowledgments

This book would not have been possible without the generosity of many people. First and foremost, we want to thank the hundreds of research participants who over the past fifteen years have allowed us into their space (often their homes) and have opened up to us. Thank you for sharing your insights; it has been a pleasure to watch you become aware of and put into words something most of us do on a daily or weekly basis but rarely truly give thought to: our experiences of news use.

Our deep gratitude goes out to the students who have directly or indirectly contributed to our various research projects. Thank you for your hard work and dedication. Because by now you are too many to name here, we have listed each of the students involved in the different projects in the Appendix. Thank you also for keeping us in the loop about your experiences on the social media platforms du jour; you keep us "young"! We also thank our (international) colleagues (most notably from Norway, Sweden, Finland, Spain, the UK, and Denmark) for inspiring us through our lively discussions and your perceptive comments.

This book would not have materialized without Bob Franklin's enthusiastic support throughout the entire process, from initiation to completion. Your unwavering energy and enthusiasm have kept ours up as well. Thank you also to Priscille: having you stay on top of things made this process much easier.

We thank the parties that have generously contributed to the various research projects that form the heart of this book: the Dutch Research Council (NWO), Dutch Journalism Fund (Stimuleringsfonds voor de Journalistiek), and Dutch news organizations (NOS Nieuws, RTL, Nieuwsuur, Buitenhof, EenVandaag, *De Volkskrant*, *Het Parool*, AD, *Trouw*, *Dagblad van het Noorden*, *Leeuwarder Courant*, EO, KRO-NRCV, VPRO, RTV Utrecht, RTV Rijnmond, Omroep West, RTV Noord-Holland, AT5, UindeWijk). We also thank the publishers and journals that have published our original work for their permission to reuse the material for this book:

Digital Journalism (Taylor & Francis), *Journalism Studies* (Taylor & Francis), *Journalism* (SAGE), and *Media, Culture & Society* (SAGE).

We also want to acknowledge the many scholars who have inspired us intellectually. These include John Dewey (experience); Elizabeth S. Bird, Sonia Livingstone and Kim Schrøder (news audiences); Nick Couldry (practice theory); Peter Dahlgren, Colin Sparks, Herbert Gans, James W. Carey, Michael Schudson and Jostein Gripsrud (popularity, democracy, and citizenship); Margaret Wetherell (discourse analysis); David Gauntlett (creative methods); and Sarah Pink (sensory and visual ethnography).

Finally, we want to thank our loved ones for their love and support. Over the years, you have encouraged us, kept us sane, and celebrated with us. To Marien (Irene) and Francys (Tim) in particular: thank you for indulging us to incessantly observe and inquire about your news and media use. You have shaped this book in more ways than you know.

1 Introduction

Changing news use, unchanged news experiences?

If media change so quickly, isn't your research always outdated?

This is the question we invariably get asked when we tell people that we study the impact of digitalization on news use. It is an understandable question: since Irene began studying news use in 2004 and Tim joined her in 2012, the devices and platforms people use for news have shifted and increased dramatically. Getting access to news has become easier than ever before; you do not necessarily have to pay for it, you can choose your own time and place, and it is only one click away. Furthermore, many people now rely on an ever-expanding number of social media (and their particular logics) to become informed, including Facebook, YouTube, Twitter, WhatsApp, Instagram, Snapchat, and TikTok. At the same time, traditional forms of news consumption took a hit: newspaper circulation numbers and linear television ratings have been falling across the board (Newman, Fletcher, Kalogeropoulos, & Nielsen, 2019). Our conversation partners reason, if the devices and platforms people rely on change and multiply, surely this means that news use has revolutionized as well?

One part of the answer is yes. The devices and platforms people use do not only change fast; they also change differently in different countries (Elvestad & Shaker, 2017). This has been well documented by the Reuters Institute of the Study of Journalism's *Digital News Report*, which since 2010 has tracked how people across the globe use news. Surveying over 75,000 people in 38 countries, it is "the most comprehensive ongoing comparative study of news consumption in the world" (Nielsen, 2019, p. 5). This raises the questions: What is there left to add about changing news use? How can we compete with such an overwhelming amount of quantitative and qualitative data?

We argue, however, that we don't compete: we answer different questions and we answer them with different approaches and methods. First, although we are interested in changing news use, our emphasis is less on news consumption itself (e.g. frequency and time spent) than on people's *experience* of their news use. After all, the object – news use – does not exist independently of its experience, and to make sense of experience, context and language matter. For instance, although many people encounter news on Facebook, this does not necessarily tell us something about (as we will show in the following chapters) *how* they actually engage with it and what it means to them. Second, our large-scale qualitative research enables us an exceptional level of depth, allowing for layered results, uncovering complexity, and paradoxes. This large amount of data (see the Appendix for an overview) enabled us to triangulate but also to crystallize research results (Costera Meijer, 2016). In contrast to triangulation, the goal of crystallization is "not to provide researchers with a more valid singular truth, but to open up a more complex, in-depth, but still thoroughly partial understanding of the issue" (Tracy, 2010, p. 844). And finally, our methodological pluralism is aimed at capturing and making sense of news use holistically: people's multi-dimensional experience, including "embodied, practical, emotional, spatial, social, linguistic, and temporal aspects" (Wertz et al., 2011, p. 127). Our phenomenological approach to news use enables us to "meaningfully illuminate *the person's world*, including experiences in the same or other persons' mental lives" (Wertz et al., 2011, p. 126, emphasis original).

Combined, our approach enables a second answer to the question that opened this chapter: it's complicated. What we argue throughout this book is that while news user practices are continuously *diversifying* (see Chapter 2), many underlying patterns of news experience – how people appreciate news – are surprisingly durable. Case in point is the surprise on our first year Media and Journalism students' faces when they realize how much they recognize themselves in the pre-social media, pre-smartphone experiences of young people (aged 15–25) described 15 years ago in Irene's 2006 book *De Toekomst van het Nieuws* (The Future of News). Although what counts as news has since broadened and the range of platforms and devices has multiplied and diversified, our current students still share a "world" with a previous generation, a world which can be characterized by a particular user attitude and an explanation about why and how they do or do not use particular news. The main attitude in 2004–2005 was that news was considered very important but not always interesting, which was offered as the main reason they did not use it often. The subtext was that being young meant enjoying oneself, and enjoyment and news consumption didn't and (paradoxically) also *shouldn't* go together: when asked if they wanted news to become more entertaining, young people were very much against this. Making news more popular would, in their eyes, affect journalism's reliability, which in turn would undermine their intention to use it. What they did use were more popular newsy programs, but they did not consider these programs real, serious news. They used them for entertainment purposes. This so-called double viewing paradox (see Costera Meijer, 2006, 2007, 2008) is still present in the personal world of our current students. Indeed, even the importance both 2004 and 2020 journalism students attach to journalism – so much so that they want to make a living out of it – is not necessarily reflected in the amount of news they consume.

A similarly stable aspect of young people's world is their need for connection. Although the Dutch platforms and devices used by the 2004–2005 students (MSN, dial-up modems, Hyves[1]) generate laughter and nostalgia among the 2020 students, both groups want, above all, to feel connected – and news plays a role in this. For journalism to be used, being informative is not enough; even more important is that it gives rise to conversations so that it ties in with people's communication patterns. This relatively unchanged news experience of young people (2004–2020) illustrates the main point of this book: while the media landscape may indeed be ever changing and people's *practices* are diversifying, insights based on a continuous stream of audience research illustrate that the way news functions in people's lives and how they experience it, including their *needs* and *pleasures*, are more stable than is often assumed.

Professional attention to changing news use

Until the beginning of the second decade of the 21st century, journalists often considered reckoning with audiences' preferences unnecessary and, indeed, uncouth, because it conflicted with their editorial independence (Coddington, 2015; Costera Meijer, 2001; Schlesinger, 1978). In "deciding what's news," journalists stated they relied primarily on their instinct, their nose for news (Gans, 1979). Fast-forward some decades and the separation between editorial rooms and business activities has all but disintegrated (Cornia, Sehl, & Nielsen, 2020). One of the perhaps unexpected by-products of the digitalization of journalism is that being responsive to audiences by editorial departments has fairly quickly become part of journalists' routines (Tandoc, 2019). Having to deal with a constant influx of audience metrics is seen as "a prerequisite for organizational adaptation to an increasingly challenging environment" (Cornia et al., 2020, pp. 172–173). Since audience metrics have become pervasive forces for commercial and public service media, paying attention to the usage patterns of audiences has become crucial for the survival of journalism (Myllylahti, 2019). Research also shows that even if they do not explicitly have to maximize users' attention by generating as many clicks, attention minutes, or shares as possible, journalists are still drawn to them (Hanusch, 2017; Karlsson & Clerwall, 2013; Usher, 2013). Some journalists tend to take these figures as representative of user preferences and proudly show their most read, viewed, and shared items (Boesman & Costera Meijer, 2018). And vice versa, although they may recognize the limitations of metrics, journalists can become demoralized about the worth of their work when it does not do "well" (Cohen, 2019).

Initially, metrics like clicks seemed to confirm some of the worst assumptions journalists entertained about their audiences. Long convinced that the general public is mostly interested in insignificant matters – as illustrated by a TV producer who argued that "they only want to know how the astronauts shit while they are in space" (Gans, 1979, p. 235) – clicking patterns seemed to indicate that people are more interested in so-called junk news than in public interest news (Boczkowski & Mitchelstein, 2013; Welbers et al., 2016), illustrating a gap between journalists' dedication to providing serious, important news and audiences' interests in trivial, fun news. However, as Cherubini and Nielsen concluded in 2016 (p. 7), "an earlier period of skepticism seems to have given way to interest in how data and metrics can help newsrooms reach their target audiences and do better journalism." In Chapters 3 and 4 we will provide more in-depth knowledge about the meaning of clicks and time spent from a user perspective. This knowledge might help journalists to better combine the information from audience metrics with their professional intuition (Zamith, 2018). Also, recent evidence pointing to quantified audiences as an increasingly important element within the formation of citizen-oriented as well as consumer-oriented role orientations (Belair-Gagnon, Zamith, & Holton, 2020) underlines the importance of more in-depth understandings of how to read audience metrics from a user perspective.

While journalists appear to become more enthusiastic about audience metrics as a form of audience feedback they can use to improve the quality of their work (Belair-Gagnon et al., 2020), some users develop counterreactions against the commercial exploitation and manipulation of their time and attention. They lament superficial, inaccurate, and sensationalist news designed to make them click (Nielsen & Graves, 2017). They install ad blockers, use applications to limit their screen use, or opt for a digital detox (Bauwens, Thorbjornsson, & Verstrynge, 2019; Neverla & Trümper, 2019; Syvertsen, 2017; Syvertsen & Enli, 2019). Some who experience news overload or who feel that news negatively influences their quality of life even choose to avoid news altogether (Brennen, 2019; Park, 2019; Woodstock, 2014). It seems, then, that while journalists are becoming more responsive to their audiences, users don't necessarily appreciate how this audience responsiveness manifests.

We argue that a genuine audience turn is needed that replaces "how to *reach* people" with "how to be of *service* to them." A genuine audience turn means moving beyond the excesses and simplified logics of the attention economy and finding alternative ways to investigate and become sensitive to the practices, preferences, and pleasures of audiences. What they appreciate may not always be derived from the *content* of journalism but resides in the *experience* it invokes in the user. As we will argue in the final chapter of this book, it may be time to replace audience responsiveness with audience sensitivity.

Theoretical framework: practices and pleasures

Because audience metrics may misrepresent what news audiences appreciate about news (as we will show in Chapters 3 and 4), it is important to investigate news user practices and pleasures with different research methods and in more detail. This may provide a more layered picture of people's news use, allowing room for ambivalence and paradoxes. For the studies that form the heart of this book, we benefited from the phenomenological principles of practice theory as background for our studies, because it enables media scholars to "recognise the variety, importance and complexity of the many new things we are doing with digital media" (Cammaerts & Couldry, 2016). Practice theory can help to make sense of whatever people are doing with news while being alert to material, technological, and sensory aspects of media use. In our research we investigate user practices through the language and discourses people employ for their everyday actions with media, platforms, and devices (e.g. via think-aloud protocols, day-in-the-life method), even when (initially) they do not have words for these actions (e.g. via video-ethnography, mood boards). This use of more naturalistic sources of data (Potter & Hepburn, 2005) enabled us to move beyond the more functionalistic uses and gratifications of news media (Blumler & Katz, 1974; Ruggiero, 2000). The concept of "requisite variety" (Ashby, 1991; Gallagher, Kaiser, Simon, Beath, & Goles, 2010) is used as starting point, referring to choosing a varied set of methods (quantitative and qualitative) to match the complexity of the investigated phenomenon. Honoring the complexity of news user practices also requires us to allow doubt into the research process in combination with the use of research strategies like triangulation, crystallization, and thick description (Costera Meijer, 2016).

Practices

Following Couldry (2011), we will investigate people's everyday experiences with news, rather than their opinions. How news use is changing cuts, in the words of Couldry (2011, p. 217), "across how people actually understand the practices in which they are engaged. And it insists we look very closely at the categorizations of practice that people themselves make, 'in practice' as it were." Taking a phenomenological approach translates into asking open questions about what people are doing with news and how they categorize this themselves (cf. Wertz et al., 2011). Such an approach is valuable because it avoids preconceptions about what counts as "news" and what counts as "doing." A more open, "non-news-centric approach" (see Chapter 5) enabled us to see how users make different genre classifications of news and journalism than professionals do, and may also consider talk shows, satire, reality TV, or consumer service information as journalism (Costera Meijer, 2006, 2007, 2008; Edgerly & Vraga, 2019). In addition, a practice approach made us aware of more passive practices such as "glancing" or "hearing" (see Chapter 2).

A focus on practices and how people experience them also fits within a non-representational and non-media-centric approach to media use (Couldry, 2012; Moores, 2012). Taking these approaches means paying attention not only to what people do *with* journalism but also *in* and *around* journalism (Couldry, 2004, 2011). For instance, when one of our participants comes home from work, she turns on a Netflix series on her TV in the background while checking news sites on her laptop. On both media, glances and moments of intense focus are alternated. She explained that the TV shows feel like a warm blanket from under which she can safely peek into or have a sense of connection with the "serious" public world. Taking into account the context, habits, feelings, and mood beyond her interpretation of the news content allows for a fuller understanding of her news use.

We argue that when studying everyday news use, it is necessary to also emphasize a second advantage of taking a non-news-centric approach. When in 2004–2005 we tried to understand what may make news more interesting to young people, it proved to be a dead end to ask them directly. "News is important, but . . ." was the standard answer we got, even from journalism students. What proved to be more revealing was asking them about informative programs (not necessarily considered "news") they found interesting or even captivating (see Costera Meijer, 2006, 2016). Those answers provided useful clues for news organizations aiming to become relevant to young people. A third reason for a non-news-centric approach is that news has become all but completely interwoven with other types of information; for instance, when doing a "checking cycle" (Chapter 2) on their smartphone, people check news sites or apps, social media, dating apps, and so on all in one go. Likewise, in social media news feeds, news is but one among many different information types. As a result, especially newer forms of digital news use can no longer be investigated in their "pure," isolated form (see Chapter 5).

One specific contribution of non-representational and non-media-centric approaches to studying media is the emphasis on how material, technological, and sensory aspects of media practices are central to processes of mediation (Pink, 2015). While news consumers tend to be implicitly conceived of as disembodied, cognitive beings whose devices and platforms are neutral conduits of information, paying attention to the material and sensory experiences is increasingly considered necessary to fully understand changing news practices (Boczkowski et al., 2020; Fortunati et al., 2015). As we will show in Chapter 5, the experience of journalism is of course always related to content, but it is also shaped by its material form, its technological features, and its sensory aspects.

An additional advantage of practice theory is its emphasis on non-essentialism. For example, people's experiences of technology and their affordances depend partly on their "perception" (awareness) and "dexterity" (knowledge) (Davis & Chouinard, 2016). Technologies mediate our practices by enabling some actions and constraining others, but different people can also use, manipulate, and interpret technologies in different ways (Ihde, 2008; Rosenberger & Verbeek, 2015). For example, some participants feel blocked in their news consumption when they hit an online paywall that indicates they have reached the maximum number of free articles per month. Other more tech-savvy participants instead know they have unlimited free access if they open news article URLs in an anonymous browser. This example illustrates the relevance of taking personal news practices as the point of departure for making sense of how news users experience and interact with their news media as material objects.

Another example of the advantage of non-essentialism is the refusal to "infer deep essential qualities on the basis of surface appearance" (Rothbart & Taylor, 1992, p. 12). For example, the practice of avoiding news is sometimes attributed to a particular group of people, called "news avoiders," while (as we will discuss in Chapter 2) in everyday life, avoiding news can also be seen as an activity everyone is involved in from time to time. While the category of "news avoider" exists statistically (Ksiazek et al., 2010), without being supplemented with an understanding of *how* and *why* people avoid news, it may conceal as much as it reveals (Groot Kormelink, 2019). For instance, Toff and Palmer (2019) found that caretakers have little time and energy left for news consumption, raising the question of whether "news avoidance" is an accurate or appropriate term here. Illustrating how a practice-based approach reduces the risk of essentialism, we will show the variety of practices of news use one person may engage in at different moments (Chapter 2).

The risk of essentializing is also present within metrics: a news user's action (e.g. a click) is either registered or not (see Groot Kormelink, 2019). Subsequently, these registrations of a singular dimension of people's news use or non-use lead to inferences about their interests and preferences (Boczkowski & Mitchelstein, 2013; Schaudt & Carpenter, 2009; Tenenboim & Cohen, 2015). The prevalence of this binary logic within the news industry may seem understandable: user actions (clicking, sharing) generate income or attention, while the absence thereof typically does not. However, our interviews with users revealed that metrics cannot be taken at face value. For instance, non-clicking (untraceable by clicks/page views) may not refer to lack of interest in the content: headlines providing important information in a condensed form are appreciated *because* users do not have to click on them. Even – or especially – for news organizations, then, the question of what metrics actually measure and what they cannot measure is urgent. We deal with this question in Chapters 3 and 4.

Pleasures

We argue that in order to understand changing news use, it is also crucial to explore the role of pleasure. While there is ample research studying the effects of news content and form on people's enjoyment of news (e.g. Grabe et al., 2000, 2003; Hendriks Vettehen et al., 2008; Lang et al., 2005), pleasure itself is seldom investigated as an appreciated part of the experience of news. It is associated with entertainment, a genre which – in spite of the many calls to abandon the opposition – is still usually considered as journalism's Other. Why this is the case falls outside the spectrum of this book (see Costera Meijer, 2021a, 2021b), but that pleasure is an intrinsic part of news use is demonstrated by our informants time and again.

Almost 30 years ago, Dahlgren and Sparks (1992) called for a renewed self-understanding of journalism, which included laying "aside the bipolar thinking which posits that against the rational/serious stands only the irrational/frivolous, and that the latter is commercially successful largely to the extent that the traditional goals of journalism are abandoned" (p. 18). Journalism, they suggested,

> must become sensitive to and acknowledge such aspects as the multiple subjectivities of everyday life, the protean purposes and diverse pleasures which people can associate with journalism, the processes by which audiences become communities of publics, the polysemy of texts, the special qualities of the television medium and the particular ways of knowing associated with narrative.
>
> (Dahlgren & Sparks, 1992, pp. 18, 19)

Similarly, Glasser (2000) called for more study of "enjoyment of news use." He argued that our everyday news use cannot only be explained by rational, utilitarian, extrinsic, and other instrumental motivations. It is therefore important to also understand why the reading, watching, listening, checking, and other practices of news use are appealing in themselves. For instance, in his classic study, Berelson (1949, p. 124) showed that when newspaper deliverymen were on strike, people missed not only the provision of information itself but also its intrinsic pleasure, "the act of reading itself . . . without primary regard for the content of the reading."

To date, journalism studies has provided an insufficient framework to study and explain changing news use, which is why we borrow concepts from neighboring disciplines to better make sense of it (see Costera Meijer, 2020a). Insights from information studies taught us how important it is to differentiate between what users recognize as *being* informed (they receive information or news) and the impact of their use: whether they actually *feel* informed or not (Bruce et al., 2014). Feeling informed is a pleasurable experience, referring to intense sensations such as "finally understanding something," "receiving recognition for one's situation," or "learning something new" (Groot Kormelink & Costera Meijer, 2017). This experience can be better worded by concepts developed in entertainment studies and narrative studies. These studies distinguish for instance between the pleasures of attention and arousal (leading to diversion or distraction) and the pleasures of satisfaction, appreciation, and transportation (e.g. Bartsch & Schneider, 2014; Green & Brock, 2000; Oliver & Bartsch, 2010; Roth et al., 2014). Media studies and human-computer interaction studies provided us with a subtler repertoire to understand the role of apparatus, platforms, devices, and algorithmic logics for our experience of news (Courtois et al., 2013; Fortunati et al., 2015; van Dijck & Poell, 2013; Ytre-Arne, 2011) as well as the pleasures involved in using technology itself, such as increasing your knowledge and skills, self-expression, sharing intimate interactions with others, and recalling memories (Hassenzahl & Tractinsky, 2006; Bargas-Avila & Hornbaeck, 2011). All these concepts help us to understand and to articulate when people derive pleasure from journalism and – just as important – when not. These insights call for more attention to the platform and device-specificness of news experiences (Chapters 2 and 5).

In short, as Christensen et al. (2012) suggest, understanding the experience of pleasure by news users – and how it relates to time, place, need, habit, mood, and platform – provides important clues for supplying a service people may pay for in attention and/or money (Chapter 6).

Research approach

This book takes an empirical look at changing news use. It focuses on the various practices people are involved in when using journalism and the

pleasures inherent to these practices. Drawing from creative methodological approaches inspired by divergent scholars such as Latour (2005), Bryant
and Charmaz (2007), Gauntlett (2007, 2011), Tracy (2010), Holstein and
Gubrium (2003), Wetherell et al. (2001), Bloor et al. (2001), and Booth
et al. (2003), and using as point of departure the concept of requisite variety (Gallagher et al., 2010; Tracy, 2010), our approach to conducting news
audience research was to select for each research question a method (or
combination of methods) that would answer it as precisely as possible. If
such a method was not available (which was the case when we wanted to
study news user practices our respondents were not aware of and were thus
unable to verbalize), we developed one: a two-sided video-ethnography
(see Chapter 5). We will introduce our methodological approach in this section in general and will go into more detail to explain which methods and
approaches were considered appropriate to answer the different research
questions in the following chapters.

First, a concrete example may illustrate the added value of our phenomenological, qualitative approach to survey research. People are asked the
question: "You say you've used these sources of news [referring to a previous question regarding people's use of particular platforms, TV, radio,
newspapers, social media etc. for news] in the last week. Which would you
say is your MAIN source of news?"[2] This question seems fairly straightfor-
ward and useful to compare people's use of various sources. But when context and language are taken into account, the answer to this question may be
less easy to make sense of. For instance, if people interpret the word "main"
in terms of frequency, then a particular news app or social platform may be
chosen as answer. If, however, they take "main" to mean "most influential"
or "most valuable," users may choose a different answer category, such as
the weekend paper they read only on Saturday morning, a weekly TV show
or podcast, or even the biweekly free local paper that informs them about
what is going on in their neighborhood. Using these forms of journalism
took up a fraction of the time they spend on news each week, but they were
nevertheless valued more. In this book we take such complexities and paradoxes into account as part of life and try to make sense of them.

A second, related characteristic of our methodological approach is aimed
at preventing a priori conclusions about what news use means to people. For
instance, while the uses and gratifications developed in the 1960s and '70s
(Katz et al., 1973; Ruggiero, 2000) – such as information, communication,
and entertainment – have remained relevant to this day, what it *means* when
people frequently use news for communicative or entertainment purposes
is rarely investigated. For instance, the dominance of light or entertainment
news in "most read" lists is often seen as evidence that people prefer or
are mostly interested in such news and thus less in "public interest" news

(e.g. Boczkowski & Mitchelstein, 2013; Schaudt & Carpenter, 2009; Tenenboim & Cohen, 2015). However, using news for communicative or entertainment gratifications may not mean that one lacks interest in news about "important" topics about current affairs. Also, the latter more often involves news user practices that don't require a click and therefore cannot easily be traced (see Chapters 2 and 3). And vice versa, the consumption of funny, stupid, and bizarre news items may not be interpreted as a sign of their value or importance to the user.

Another example of how a particular use of news can be misinterpreted is provided by 23-year-old beauty blogger Jorien. When we tracked her news use, she showed a clear interest in fashion and lifestyle, which we initially interpreted as an entertaining experience similar to the experience of other women in this tracking study who visited the same types of websites (Kleppe & Costera Meijer, 2015; Kleppe & Otte, 2017). When we interviewed her later, she explained how she engaged in a practice we call "scanning" (Chapter 2). Scanning is about efficiently seeing whether there are any new developments one should know about regarding news that is – in this case – of vital importance to you. For Jorien, www.misslipgloss.nl and www.beautylab.nl were *news* sources that fulfill an information need related to her professional interests: as a beauty blogger, she wants to be updated not only as quickly as possible but also with reliable, good-quality beauty information.

By analyzing people's news use in their own context, we try to find and name more precisely how news functions in their world. This includes moving beyond the functional emphasis of uses and gratifications theory by also taking seriously non-functional, taken-for-granted aspects of news use: pleasures, such as creating a moment for oneself or the joy of finding a fresh, crisp newspaper on your doormat (Chapters 2 and 5); displeasures, such as the frustration when a news video doesn't load properly (Chapter 4); and mixed emotions, such as being gleefully annoyed by a headline about someone you don't like (e.g. schadenfreude when reading news about Donald Trump) (Chapter 3).

Third, and in line with calls for more naturalistic sources of data (Potter & Hepburn, 2005; Wertz et al., 2011) to make sense of the specific character of news use, we observed in real-life contexts (and sometimes in real time) the everyday news use activities of hundreds of people (in-depth interviews, day-in-the-life method). The think-aloud protocol (van den Haak et al., 2003) proved to be particularly useful to get a grip on audience metrics from "the other side," as user experiences (Chapters 3 and 4). To understand the preferences of news users for particular forms of storytelling, selection, and presentation of news we employed in-depth interviews, focus groups, and street intercept interviews. To extend our knowledge about the oft-ignored material and sensory dimensions of everyday news use, employing a video-ethnography worked out well, in particular for those experiences research participants were able to reflect on only when shown the visual material of their own news practices.

In keeping with our phenomenological approach, we analyzed over 1,000 accounts (transcripts of recorded conversations and video recordings) as "language in use" and "human meaning-making" (Wetherell et al., 2001, p. 3) rather than as signs to what might be "beyond" them. In our focus on what people are doing with news, we focus on the language as it is used by the informants or research participants and present this in their own words rather than paraphrased. Some participants were interviewed multiple times between 2012 and 2020, allowing us not only to compare news use between people but also to see how it changes in the course of people's lives.

From audience responsive to audience sensitive

This book provides scholars, journalists and news organizations with insights to become more sensitive to the needs and the wants of news users. As noted, we argue that while news user practices (including their material, sensory, and habitual dimensions) are diversifying, the pleasures that people derive from the use of news and how news fits into their lifeworld prove to be more durable than one might expect in a quickly changing media landscape. We argue that being sensitive to users' experiences rather than being responsive to their (apparent) interests and preferences may be a way to build a more lasting and constructive relationship with one's audience. Instead of assuming that what people use most frequently (*frequency fallacy*) or spend most time on (*duration fallacy*) can be read as what they find most interesting or even most important, we propose an attitude of sensitivity which centers on listening to and understanding real people's needs for journalism (see Costera Meijer, 2021b). The notion of audience sensitivity may function as a necessary addition to or even an alternative for audience responsiveness (e.g. Anderson, 2011b; Brants & de Haan, 2010; de Haan, 2012). Developing audience sensitivity means that journalists become aware of and sensitive to what people truly appreciate about journalism and in particular to the infrastructure behind this: what, when, where, and how the audience wants to pay attention or money for day-to-day news and in-depth journalism. Audience sensitivity as a professional value and attitude also contains a critical edge, such as a sense of caution and prudence regarding what the public wants or regarding what their abstract representations (user metrics, circulation figures, ratings, or shares) suggest they want. We expand on this idea in Chapter 6.

Outline of the book

In Chapter 2 we explore what has changed in people's news consumption by comparing patterns in news use between 2004 and 2020. We identify 24 distinct practices of news use: reading, watching, viewing, glancing, listening, hearing, checking, snacking, scanning, monitoring, searching, clicking, saving, scrolling, triangulating, avoiding, abstaining, linking, sharing, liking, recommending, commenting, voting, and tagging. These distinct user practices challenge the generally taken-for-granted automatic link between media platforms, media technology, and news consumption.

In Chapter 3 we focus on one practice of news use: clicking. The chapter problematizes the relationship between clicks, user preferences, and the audience's interests. Journalists and journalism scholars often interpret these clicking patterns as evidence that news users are mostly interested in junk news, leading to concerns about the state of journalism and the vitality of democracy. Through observing and asking how users actually browse news and what clicking and not clicking mean to them, we identify 30 distinct considerations for clicking and not clicking, classifying them into three categories: cognitive, affective, and pragmatic. The results suggest that clicks are a flawed instrument to measure interest. It is too crude a term to account for the variety of people's considerations for (not) clicking, not in the least because an absence of clicking does not mean people lack interest in this news.

In Chapter 4 we problematize a second dominant audience metric: time spent. The amount of time people spend on news is often taken for granted by scholars and news organizations as a degree of user involvement and audience interests. Exploring what spending time with news means from an audience perspective, we will show how time spent does not necessarily measure interest in, attention to, or engagement with news: first, time spent does not reflect the quality of attention being paid; second, there is no linear relationship between time spent and interest or engagement; third, different news devices, platforms, and genres coincide with different temporal experiences of news.

Chapter 5 captures the material and sensory dimensions of everyday news use that tend to be ignored. We developed a two-sided video-ethnography to tap into news users' embodied, tacit knowledge. Our findings illustrate how the materiality of devices and platforms and the ways users physically handle and navigate them impact how they engage with news, in ways they themselves had not realized. The chapter also shows how people actively "make" place and time through their news practices, using coping strategies that mediate between the comfortability of ritual news use and the disruptiveness of news content.

In our final chapter, we discuss how news organizations and journalists can reckon with news users' needs and wants beyond audience metrics. We suggest a shift from audience responsiveness to audience sensitivity. If news organizations want to move beyond the simplified logics and excesses of the attention economy, they have to find alternative ways to become sensitive to and investigate the needs and preferences of audiences/users. Getting more knowledgeable about what audiences appreciate about their news user practices seems a good starting point. This chapter applies the knowledge gained in the previous chapters to address the productiveness and usefulness of becoming *audience sensitive* to news media and journalism scholars.

Notes

1 At the time an extremely popular social platform similar to Myspace and Facebook.
2 An extract from the 2020 questionnaire of Reuters Digital News Report.

2 Scrolling, triangulating, tagging, and abstaining

The diversification of news use between 2004 and 2020[1]

In 2014, we investigated the widely held proposition that news use was changing at a rapid pace. At the time, Purcell, Rainie, Mitchell, Rosenstiel, and Olmstead (2010) identified three drastic shifts: (1) from news consumed in fixed places and at fixed times to mobile news consumed at moments selected by the user; (2) from generalized news to customized news, tailored to the user's individual desires and needs; and (3) from news consumed passively by users to news to which they actively contribute. The digitalization of journalism was said to have enabled news to evolve from a genre of information into a social experience (Hermida, Fletcher, Korell, & Logan, 2012).

We argued that these claims may have overstated the extent of changes in the nature of news use. First, the studies usually relied on survey- or diary-based inquiries in which respondents report their own news consumption. People, however, have the tendency to overestimate their own news use. Prior (2009) found that people over age 55 estimate their television news use twice as high, and young people (aged 18–34) even eight times as high. Araujo, Wonneberger, Neijens, and de Vreese (2017), comparing self-reported internet use and tracking data, similarly found that people tend to overestimate the time they spend online.

Second, these overestimations, in turn, may fall victim to the "frequency fallacy," or the misconception that what people use most frequently can be read as what they most appreciate or find most important, and vice versa, that what people use less frequently is automatically a sign of its lesser value or importance (cf. Tversky & Kahneman, 1983). The importance of involving context in making sense of the frequency of news use is illustrated by the response of visitors of *Cinekid*, a youth film festival in Europe. Irene was invited to give a lecture at the festival because of the publication of her book about young people's news use (Costera Meijer, 2006). After she introduced her main results – among them their diminishing frequency of news usage – some youngsters reacted angrily. They did not believe the statistical evidence (shares and ratings) or the qualitative explanations of young people quoted in the book. At the time Irene could not make sense of their reaction. Why would young, critical, societally involved people dismiss the results of sound academic research so easily? These fuming youngsters were adamant they used news "every day," which could be true, but this feeling of "frequent news use" might also be the result of their finding news important and therefore overrating their use. In hindsight, introducing the frequency fallacy may have helped in the communication.

Equally relevant today, as metrics (click, time spent) have become a dominant measure of news use, is the "duration fallacy," or the misconception that the amount of time people spend on news can be read as a sign of what they find most important. Here context matters too. Just like how spending more time with colleagues or classmates does not mean they are more important than loved ones, spending more time with news is not automatically a sign of its value or importance (see Chapters 3 and 4).

We therefore focus on what people are actually *doing* with news and what this *means* to them. Following Couldry (2011), we investigated news use as a particular range of practices, including how news usage interacts with other social and cultural practices. This chapter updates the 2014 article and adds eight additional news user practices. We limit our analysis to practices related to the everyday consumption of individual news products (news bulletin, newspaper, news site, news app, news item, etc.), thereby excluding practices such as subscribing, following, or contributing to news.

Putting news use into words: aim and methodology

This chapter is based on a synthesizing analysis of 23 multi-method research projects carried out over a period of 15 years and focused on tracing what people do with news and what this means to them (see the Appendix). It explores what has changed in people's news consumption by comparing patterns in news use between 2004–2005 and 2011–2020. The objective is twofold. First, it answers more precisely the question about how practices of news use have changed reflecting the digitalization of news and the introduction of social media. Second, it aims to expand and deepen the existing professional and academic vocabulary about journalism from the perspective of the user. The "newsroom-centricity of journalism ethnography" (Wahl-Jorgensen, 2009) has generated an extensive terminology for discussing news production, but the repertoire for the analysis and description of news usage is mostly limited to reading, watching, checking, listening, clicking, or sharing news.

As we argued in Chapter 1, to show how news use has changed we take as the starting point not people's opinions but their everyday experiences and how they "actually understand the practices in which they are engaged" (Couldry, 2004, p. 121). The value of asking open questions about what people are doing with news and how they categorize this themselves lies in avoiding scholarly preconceptions about what counts as "news" and what counts as "doing." When discussing "real" or "quality" news, people's definitions are similar to professional ones and center around news about civic issues that provides background and can be trusted (Van Damme, 2020), but their experience of journalism (a broader category) also includes talk shows, satire, consumer programs, and current affairs shows (Costera Meijer, 2006; Edgerly & Vraga, 2019).

Over the past 15 years, our studies of news use have generated a vocabulary grounded in the everyday news practices of readers, viewers, and listeners. To track down these practices, several creative methods were employed to stimulate narrative production (Charmaz, 2006; Gauntlett, 2007; Holstein & Gubrium, 2003). The audience studies of 2004–2005 and 2011–2020 (see Appendix) included a wide variety of methods: quantitative surveys and digital news tracking, diaries, focus groups, and in-depth interviews which included the think-aloud protocol (Ericsson & Simon, 1993; van den Haak, De Jong, & Jan Schellens, 2003), day-in-the-life method (Del Rio Carral, 2014), mood boards (McDonagh, Bruseberg, & Haslam, 2002), ranking exercises, sensory ethnography (Pink, 2009), and video-ethnography (see Chapter 5). These approaches were designed to *dis*courage the research participants from giving an *opinion* about news – their default mode – while *en*couraging them to articulate what they were *doing* with news and their *experience* of it. For instance, using the day-in-your-life method, participants were asked to take the researcher through a typical day of news use: "Imagine it's morning, your alarm goes off. What is the first moment you encounter news?," followed repeatedly by "What is the next moment you encounter news?" Going through their day chronologically allowed participants to envisage their news use, resulting in a vivid account of their news routines. A second example is the street interviews about news avoidance. Consciously downplaying the status of the research by introducing it as "a school project," the interviewer drew attention to this issue by asking passersby: "For a school project, I am looking for people who are not concerned with news or even avoid it. Do you recognize yourself in this?" By inviting people to express their personal experience with news avoidance (recognizing a practice) instead of asking them to provide their opinion about the topic, the interviewer managed to get people ($N = 240$) to talk about how the practice did or did not fit in their own life (Zumpolle, 2017).

Centering our approaches explicitly around participants' own practices enabled them to access and communicate their experiences of everyday news use (Groot Kormelink, 2020). Underlying user configurations were detected by applying the interpretative repertoire analysis first developed by Potter and Wetherell (1987). This approach is aimed at discovering discursive patterns used by speakers to interpret their daily life and to describe and explain their considerations, decisions, and behavior.

Ultimately, in this chapter 24 practices of news use are identified. News users themselves described their different forms of news use as *activities*, which could be labeled as verbs. While they did not always use the exact same terms, our informants distinguished the following user practices: reading, watching, viewing, glancing, listening, hearing, checking, snacking, scanning, monitoring, searching, clicking, saving, scrolling, triangulating, avoiding, abstaining, linking, sharing, liking, recommending, commenting, voting, and tagging. To develop a vocabulary "from the inside," these different practices will be illustrated in the words of users themselves. Rather than representing individual points of view, the quotations derived from our research are used to be illustrative of common practices among news users. Some quotes may be slightly edited for readability.

Reading

The term "reading" usually serves as a catch-all for a variety of activities, such as the reading of books, magazines, newspapers, websites, and apps. When it comes to journalism, however, our research participants give reading a more specific meaning. Reading is about depth: it is done individually, with great attention, and (when users have enough time) in longer sessions. Often, reading as a particular practice of news use is less about *knowing* that something occurred than about *understanding* a news event. As with novels, people read when they feel relaxed and have time to do it in a concentrated fashion, and they return to it when they have enough time or feel at ease. Fien (56) reads her daily newspaper before going to bed, when she can "*really* read in peace, with a glass of wine, just *really* concentrated." Reading is about immersion. As Fien explained: "You can pick up the newspaper again and focus once more on that complicated piece of text when it's convenient to you or when it is easier to concentrate."

In 2004, the research participants used the word "reading" mainly in relation to their use of printed newspapers. Although 15 years later, reading as an attentive news practice remains unchanged, it has become less tied to one platform. Our research results support Rosenstiel's (2013) assertion that the digitalization of journalism has not only led to a decline in reading habits. News is read increasingly in digital formats, on computers, laptops, and tablets, and even on smartphones, as illustrated by Rob (28), who reads Longreads before going to sleep: "During the day, it seems, I don't take the time for that." Indeed, while in 2014 it was still fairly uncommon for our participants to read long-form news on smartphones, by 2020 this is no longer exceptional.

Watching

In terms of intensity, watching news is akin to reading but also to the active, lean-forward spectator mode of the cinematic experience. When research participants described their news use in terms of watching, they referred to it as a fairly intense practice. The news has your full attention and you do not want to be disrupted or bothered by distractive talk in the same room. In 2004–2005, watching was described as the default TV news user mode. This could be irritating, especially to younger viewers, as 21-year-old Marianne indicated:

> I still remember how I used to be annoyed by it when my parents were watching the news on TV. You had to keep silent and could ask no questions because they were watching the news, which was important for knowing what was happening in the world.

Digital TV has made it possible to watch the news in ways similar to how readers read newspapers or magazines. When they watch, they are immersed in the news and when something else demands attention, they can easily put it down (Hermes, 1995). Joan (55) puts the news on pause mode while she prepares her breakfast, after which she can continue watching when she is ready to sit down. For her, attentive news watching is like eating a decent meal: it keeps you going for some time.

Like reading, it has become much more common to watch news on the smartphone. On "lazy Sundays," Ferdinand (30) enjoys watching long-form news videos on the Vice app on his iPhone: "Like there is corruption, hate and violence in Kosovo and they really give you an in-depth view on that, like it's not just 'Oh yeah this bomb exploded in a certain building,' like they really explain what is happening."

In 2004–2005, watching the news often served in part to structure people's days (Lull, 1990). Children had to go to bed right before or right after the eight o'clock news. In 2011–2014, this structural function remained important (D'heer, Paulussen, & Courtois, 2012). However, the structural function is no longer limited to one medium: several research participants claimed to watch the eight o'clock news on their laptops, some because they no longer owned a television but still wanted a live (stream) experience; others so not to disturb the other people in the room. Portable devices have also made it possible to embed watching the news in routines outside of the home. In the morning, Dick (55) and his colleague watch the latest news bulletin on demand on his iPad together. This ritual marks the start of their workday, offers them a sociable moment, and gives them something to talk about: "It's about that coffee moment together before you really get to work. . . . I find I really enjoy that, watching the news together and afterward discussing the things that caught your eye." This joint user practice was unthinkable in 2004. Since 2014, high-speed internet and increased video performance on smartphones have made this practice even more accessible. Aside from fulfilling an informational, ritual, and communicative function, watching, like reading, also provides a moment of pleasure: people *deeply enjoy* these practices.

Viewing

Fifteen years ago, the dominant mode of television news consumption was the attentive, lean-forward activity of watching. Our more recent interviews suggest the relevance of making a distinction between watching and the volatile, relaxed, lean-back mode of *viewing* – even when the terms themselves were sometimes used interchangeably by participants in our studies. Viewing refers to its subordination to other activities. In these situations, news often functions as wallpaper for a main activity, like preparing breakfast or dinner, checking your e-mail, or reading the newspaper. Walter (35) hardly notices the TV news he puts on every morning: "They constantly repeat the news programming . . . and at some point I realize 'oh wait, I have now seen this five times' . . . and then I turn it off immediately." In Walter's case, TV news functions less as an information provider than as the soundtrack of his morning routine. For Carmen (25), an early-evening current affairs TV show similarly serves a background function when she gets home from work:

> Usually when I get home I turn on the TV and usually it begins at 06:30 p.m., I think. And then it's on in the background, but then I'm also cooking and [unpacking] the groceries, so doing all kinds of things at home, and then if it's really interesting I will watch a bit, but it's not like I think "Now I'm gonna sit down for it and now I'm really gonna watch DS."

As Carmen indicates, when the content becomes truly interesting she will temporally switch to lean-forward watching, but viewing is her default mode. It is especially lighter, easygoing TV shows (breakfast TV, talk shows, celebrity news) that lend themselves well to viewing, as Maggie (32) illustrates: "For me it's the moment just before dinner. . . . It's not brought too heavy with all kinds of calculations and things you really have to pay attention to in order to follow it."

Glancing

Glancing means subconsciously taking a brief or hurried look at news headlines, on a screen in the bus, at a kiosk, or on a homepage that contains news banners, like Yahoo.com and MSN.com. It is a "low-intensity news consumption practice" (Thurman & Fletcher, 2018, p. 1014) that is the by-effect of another activity (riding the bus, walking past a kiosk, starting up your internet browser, etc.). You notice some headlines but do not pay attention to them unless something catches your eye. On his way to the university every morning, Pere (19) – whether he wants to or not – sees the headlines of tabloid newspapers on display near the kiosk. He never consciously pays attention to them and only realized that he glances at them when one day he recognized a familiar face on the front page of one of the newspapers.

Listening

The act of *listening* to *news* has not been reflected upon much as a user practice. Even the *Handbook of Media Audiences* captures the reception of listening from a production angle (Cook, 2011). Although in 2014 there were more active forms of listening to news, such as via podcasts, our participants seldom mentioned them. This changed at the end of the second decade. The Reuters Digital News Report 2019 shows that podcasts are especially popular among younger generations (<35) and mostly listened to at home (64%), followed by public (24%) and private (20%) transport (Newman, 2019). Our informants associate listening with creating intimacy: it enables the demarcation of a personal space and being off the world for some time. Like reading, listening is about deep enjoyment: taking or even creating a moment for oneself. In the case of podcasts, this takes on an extra dimension as listening becomes "an easily customized experience" (Perks & Turner, 2019, p. 104): not only can you decide when, where, and how to listen, but you can also – much more easily than with radio – select a podcast that fits your current mood. For avid listeners, seeing a new episode of their favorite podcast in their podcast app or getting a notification feels akin to a fresh newspaper lying on the doormat: a personal treat, waiting for you to indulge yourself.

In the pre-television period, listening could be akin to reading in its intensity: people were sitting close to the device and listened intently to radio plays. While listening to a podcast (perhaps the contemporary counterpart of radio plays) is more intense than hearing, it may not be quite as intense as reading or watching because it is often combined with other activities, such as doing household chores or working out, which also demand one's partial attention. Perks and Turner (2019) argue that the gratifications associated with such multitasking are "temptation bundling" – making a mundane or boring activity (jogging, ironing) more enjoyable by simultaneously engaging in an immediately gratifying experience – and "feeding the brain." Both gratifications, as well as how listening is about taking a moment for oneself, are illustrated by our participant Tyson (29):

> Moments of mindfulness or cleaning or rest, then I put it on, especially in the evening when I'm like, I want to do something more useful, something more nourishing than just watching YouTube for instance.

Listening can also be combined with driving a car, but the driver should be able to do that on auto pilot. Sometimes, as Pim (62) told us, a radio program is so captivating that he stays in his car to continue listening even when he has reached his destination.

Hearing

The participants in our studies from 2004–2005 and 2011–2014 did not distinguish between listening and hearing; only in our most recent interviews were they recognized as distinct practices. In particular, when discussing podcasts (see previous section), research participants realized how listening is a more intense, focused activity (comparable to watching), while they experience hearing news less as an activity in its own right than as part of a more general experience, like trying to fall asleep or driving a car. The distinction can be illustrated by comparing noise to sound. While you hear a noise (passively), you listen (focused) to a sound. Hearing is done less attentively than listening and is more akin to viewing: content matters, but more important are the diversion, entertainment, and companionship it offers, and the feeling of being connected to the outside world. This is illustrated by Willie (58), who while driving always has a local news station on that plays "luckily a lot of music . . . and uh, some news in between." And Bart (35) explained how he turns on the radio on his iPad or iPhone before going to bed, but does not care whether the news is on or something else: "Whatever it is, merely some chatting or news – as long as someone is talking." If listening is more about selecting content you are in the mood for, hearing is more about *setting the mood* (Larsen, 2000).

Checking

In 2004–2005 our research participants introduced the notion of *checking* as a habitual activity, comparable to e-mail checking. It involves finding out – as efficiently as possible – whether something "new" and "interesting" has happened (Costera Meijer, 2006, 2008; Lewis, Inthorn, & Wahl-Jorgensen,

2005). Fifteen years ago, a popular news site (www.NU.nl) enabled people like Erik (25) to regularly and conveniently – in his case at least ten times a day – check if any news had been added (Costera Meijer, 2006). "It is very easy to check; you see immediately when something has happened. It hardly takes time; it is really a matter of a flash and you're gone again." The ongoing, regular urge to be on top of the latest developments seemed to be less connected to a need to be fully informed and more of an end in itself: checking is about *knowing*, not about understanding. In 2004–2005, checking was a broad label that stood for speed, no longer having to wait for the news broadcast or for the newspaper's delivery. Participants valued the convenience of 24/7 updates, the quickness, immediacy, and effortlessness, and the excitement of being on top of the news.

More than a decade later, checking as a news habit has gained in intensity. Especially news apps have made checking even quicker and more effortless. While in 2005, Erik praised the immediacy of checking news online on his computer or laptop, ten years later the quickness and effortlessness of apps have enabled the frequency of checking to go up greatly, while the activity of one click or swipe on a smartphone may be considered too laborious (for more details, see Chapter 3). In 2004–2005, checking was limited to the availability of wired internet, but today mobile devices like tablets and especially smartphones facilitate 24/7 checking. When asked how often she checks her news on her smartphone, Eva (27) laughs: "Honestly, I wouldn't be able to tell you! Because when I have a second to spare, I'll reach for my phone. [Interviewer: "Like 20 times?"] In an hour!"

In 2004–2005, checking news at work was considered a moment of pause, just like smoking a cigarette. In 2020, all micro-periods of waiting can be padded with news: in the bathroom, waiting for the elevator, at the bus stop, or between appointments. In 2004–2005, the participants in our studies checked the news on their PC or laptop and were adamant about not wanting news on their mobile phone. The frequent news alerts or push messages, inherent to getting every single news item as a text message (SMS), were experienced as too disrupting. Today, users have more control: to a large extent, they decide where and when they check the news. Checking news has become ingrained in "the interstices of the daily routine" (Dimmick, Feaster, & Hoplamazian, 2011). While they do interrupt people's activities, even push messages can be welcome, when users have signed up to be updated about breaking news.

Because of the increasingly pervasive culture of checking, news has become integrated with all sorts of activities but also with other websites and genres. A distinctive user pattern in this respect is what we have called a "checking cycle," which involves checking the latest in terms of news, e-mail, Facebook, Twitter, Instagram, Tinder, Grindr, and so on, all in one quick session. The aim is to continuously stay on top of all that happens in your personal life and the world at large. The checking cycle has an additional function at social gatherings, where it serves as a demarcation of personal space. Sebastian (39) describes how he can be sitting on the couch in the middle of a birthday party checking his smartphone, sending out the signal "I'm busy, don't disturb me." He confesses: "I like to check my mail and the socials, not because I need to but because I don't want to take part in the conversation."

Snacking

The label "snacking" was first used 15 years ago for describing a laid-back form of news consumption. Snacking is not about pursuing in-depth knowledge or developed opinions but about diversion: users consume bits and pieces of information in a relaxed, easygoing fashion to fill time while waiting for an appointment or to create a moment for oneself. In 2004–2005 some of our interviewees drew an analogy between news and a table loaded with tapas: it is impossible to eat all of it, but picking and choosing from them is delicious. A 25-year-old student:

> What I like about the different media is that you can pick up one thing and not be stuck with it; the nice thing about news is that it's volatile and always available. And because there are so many different things, it's just wonderful that you can switch back and forth between a wide variety of items.

Although snacking as a news practice has changed little since 2004–2005, like checking, it is much more widely facilitated today. On most websites and apps, users can select separate text, video, or audio fragments. In the morning, Kevin (26) picks and chooses the best bits and pieces of information from his newspaper, TV, and laptop – all simultaneously. Snacking news is a markedly more relaxed mode of news use than checking. Joost (28) snacks a news site before getting productive at work:

> There is always that moment when you haven't started to work yet and instead drink coffee and stuff like that, and then I often read NU.nl. . . . It doesn't come with a lot of depth and it really provides a kind of shoddy overview, but it still gives you a quick overview.

Snacking can be compared to user strategies such as flipping through a magazine. The point is to gather a taste of the general news and random facts in a relaxed, undemanding fashion. In snacking, the communicative value of news is often more important than its informational value. You snack news less to get informed than to have something to talk about.

In 2019, snacking was also a dominant practice on Instagram. Dianne (18) follows Dutch public broadcaster's Instagram page *NOS Stories* and appreciates the low level of effort news on Instagram demands: "[It's] just a short clip . . . and you don't have to watch it, so if I don't find it interesting I just scroll on." This aligns with Larsson's (2018) finding that on Instagram, social news users gravitate toward light and less demanding forms of interaction.

Scanning

Scanning differs from checking and snacking in that it pertains to the highlights of news in order to get the gist of the story. Rather than being up to date or getting a general impression of the news, scanning is about efficiently seeing whether there are any new developments one should know about, often within a specific domain. When scanning, users stay on the surface of a text and pick out individual words and sentences that indicate change. In 2014, Marijn (58), who has a job with a good deal of financial responsibility, *scanned* the headlines of a financial newspaper every morning, whereas he *read* a different paper for general news. Six years later, although the (paywalled) website enables him regular updates during working hours, his scanning frequency did not go up: scanning the paper once a day at breakfast is enough to feel informed. News sites that include not only headlines but also short leads on their homepage even enable users to scan without having to click. Kjell (33) illustrates: "I found that a very pleasant way of reading, that you can scan the whole [lead] without having to open the [news item]."

Scanning is about usefulness and less about pleasure. In 2004–2005, Anja (16) claimed that it was "nice when I'm able to join in the conversation about important things or when I get what people are talking about." Although the meaning of scanning has not changed much over the past 15 years, like checking and snacking it has become much easier to do. Whenever Marjolijn (25) travels between Amsterdam and Groningen on the train to visit her relatives, she will make use of the free Wi-Fi to scan her iPhone or iPad for the latest sports news and showbiz gossip. She is less interested in the content than in the shared frame of reference it provides. Scanning allows for creating common ground with the relatives she is going to meet. As she indicated, it enables her to "join in conversations rather than having to say 'oh I don't know, I don't know' all the time."

Monitoring

Schudson (1998) proposed that in order to function in a democracy, it might suffice for citizens to monitor the news instead of being fully informed. He made a striking comparison with parents watching their children in a swimming pool: they are keeping an eye out, prepared to come into action when needed. In line with this metaphor, our informants claimed to experience monitoring as actively surveying the informational environment to be able to come into action when necessary. Unlike scanning, which lacks a sense of *urgency*, monitoring is about remaining alert to emergent developments of a particular calamity which may put yourself, your family, your environment, or your fellow beings into danger. If monitoring is usually focused on one event, as a focused activity it is in some ways similar to checking and scanning, but checking serves as an end in itself (overview), while scanning serves a similar purpose but remains on the surface and includes a broader array of topics.

As a practice of news use, monitoring was not widespread in the Netherlands in the years 2004–2005. Our interviewees claimed to monitor the news only in the context of major calamities, which is understandable, because without widely available Wi-Fi it took some effort to keep an eye on events. After the 2004 earthquake in Al Hoceima (Morocco), Achmed-Amin, a 21-year-old cook's assistant from Amsterdam, invested much time in monitoring the news in an internet café for updates on the disaster in his place of birth. When in 2004 a migrant student shot his school teacher, Steven (of Indonesian descent) felt urged to monitor the events that followed: "What was important to me in that case was first the why and second the implications for Dutch society, because it involved a sensitive issue, especially in the light of my own non-native background."

Today, push messages, live blogs, social media like Twitter, and the "appification" of journalism and information have made monitoring extremely easy. People are actively invited to closely follow unfolding events that are important or appealing to them, whether it be terrorist attacks or a fugitive "Bonnie and Clyde" on their way through the Netherlands and Germany: "When those two criminals were on the loose last week, I was constantly checking my phone to see if they had been caught. It was very scary" (Annalise, 53). During the COVID-19 pandemic in 2020, people also tended to monitor the developments of the spread of the virus infection as well as the policies of various governments to restrict its diffusion and damage.

Searching

Searching is about finding an answer to a specific question, ranging from important societal issues to personal and trivial matters. In contrast to the previously described news activities, when searching users attach less value to the gatekeeping abilities of news organizations and prefer search engines. When searching, the source tends to be subordinated to the efficiency, the effort, and the time needed to find information, as Marianne (51) explains: "I go to Google and then. . . [types in search term] it doesn't really matter, I take the top [hit] to see what is going on." Indeed, Kalogeropoulos, Fletcher, and Nielsen (2018) found that news users are far less likely to correctly attribute a news story to a news brand when searching versus directly accessing a news site. This does not mean, however, that the news source becomes completely irrelevant. Marianne does have a brand preference: "Here, *De Volkskrant* (Dutch quality newspaper) on top, I don't like *De Volkskrant*, not online either. I have to admit that I often, uh, pick *De Telegraaf* (popular newspaper) if I see it listed."

If in 2004 searching was computer- and place-bound, by 2014 the "smartphonization" and "Wi-Fication" of journalism had enabled searching to become intertwined with other everyday activities, such as having dinner or watching a sports program: users will search anytime and anywhere, and will often find the information needed within seconds, even when looking for very specific or quite trivial data ("what is that singer's name again?"). Five years later, doing a quick search, or "googling," remains a pervasive practice. Google is even used for finding the homepage of news sites: interviews with young people (8–12) illustrate how despite checking the website of *Jeugdjournaal* (Dutch news program for children) on a daily basis, it was easier for them to use the search term "Jeugdjournaal" than to bookmark the website or type in the URL directly.

Clicking

Hitting news items or links for more information is a particular news habit we call *clicking*. Although this practice was around in 2004–2005, our interviewees at the time did not mention it yet in relation to news. Journalism researchers have compared clicking on news online with choosing a TV program or selecting a newspaper article (Boczkowski & Mitchelstein, 2010). On news sites users tend to click on "journalistic fast-food," as the Dutch Nieuwsmonitor (2013) found. Crime, sports news, and entertainment scored best online (with 60%) and were more often clicked on than the "important" news. Consequently, research that looks at clicking patterns is rather critical about people's scope of interests (Schaudt & Carpenter, 2009; Tenenboim & Cohen, 2015). Boczkowski and Mitchelstein (2013) even speak of a "news gap" between the news journalists produce and the news users demand.

Using the think-aloud protocol to observe people's consideration for clicking on news allowed us to distinguish two different functions of clicking: clicking on hyperlinks *within* news items and clicking on individual news items. Anne (22) illustrates how the former is tied to an informational motive: "Consider, for example, the EU: you can find what it *actually* means by clicking on it." Users value the sense of control offered by hyperlinks: by clicking, *they* decide how much (extra) information they get to see (Lagerwerf & Verheij, 2014).

Clicking on individual items, on the other hand, concerns an *additional* activity – on top of checking or snacking, for instance – that often emanates from curiosity about urgent, strange, shocking, or funny news items. This may explain why crime news is well represented in "most-read" lists. In the case of shocking or funny headlines, clicking may not be comparable to selecting a TV program or a newspaper article: it is less about choosing to invest your attention in something than about silly diversion, taking a little (mental) break. Joe (26) illustrates this well:

> Then I click it if it's a very sensational headline, so I'm more like "oh what the hell" . . . sometimes there are headlines that make you go like "what is this ridiculousness" or "what the hell is that supposed to mean," and then I'm sometimes inclined to click.

As Joe suggests, clicking on sensational headlines is about entertaining yourself with relatively useless news.

Although clicking may result in more intense forms of news use such as reading or watching, it often leads to scanning, as illustrated by the following two remarks:

> I saw that headline, "Man speeds through Amsterdam during flight from police." . . . Well, then I'm curious where that was. [clicks] In the Bijlmer [neighborhood with a bad reputation] of course, that's enough for me.
>
> (Kevin, 29)

> "Frozen from fear I could only pray, robbery of [supermarket]." Oh I didn't know there was a robbery, then I'm just gonna look which [supermarket] it was. [clicks] It's in Nieuw West [neighborhood with a bad reputation], yeah, there it happens regularly, so I'm OK.
>
> (Norah, 31)

In both cases, the informants scanned the news item with one question in mind: did this happen close to me? As soon as they saw that was not the case – it happened in areas where they would expect it – they moved on.

Moreover, contrary to what metric-based research suggests (Boczkowski & Mitchelstein, 2013; Nieuwsmonitor, 2013; Schaudt & Carpenter, 2009; Tenenboim & Cohen, 2015), the practice of *not* clicking does not automatically illustrate a lack of interest in news items. From the headlines or the lead, our interviewees generally derive sufficient information to get an impression or an update of serious events, as Marie-Claire (23) shows: "Technology [category] I always like, but usually the headlines are enough, unless I'm really like 'Huh? How can that be?'" In other words, to click or not to click does not serve as a sound standard for the level of interest or importance attached to a news item. We will elaborate on the practices of clicking and non-clicking in Chapter 3.

Saving

The term "saving" is reserved for the practice of storing news for later when one has the time to read it or archiving it for future reference. Participants save both print newspapers and digital news. The practice of saving includes quickly scanning or scrolling through an article to gauge if it is worth saving. When Ferdinand (30) saw a potentially interesting article on Facebook, he clicked on it, quickly scrolled through it and decided it was worthy of reading later due to its constructive angle: "When I saw this [section] 'what to do' [it] told me . . . that there was more depth to the news."

Various news sites and apps enable users to save news items, and apps like Pocket and Instapaper allow users to save web pages with one click and send them to their phone, tablet, or computer, so they can read them later (even offline) when they have time to immerse themselves in the issues addressed. When travelling by train, Elger (26) grabs his " 'digital reading file': sometimes the items are a week old, but that doesn't really matter, because in fact it is not quite about the really hard news, but about backgrounds." Several participants did admit, though, they often do not get around to actually reading the saved items. When we interviewed Joanne (32), we noticed a pile of weekend supplements from her regional newspaper lying in a corner. When we asked about this pile in a follow-up interview, Joanne laughed and admitted she had been saving them for later but could not bring herself to actually read them.

Scrolling

Scrolling was discovered as a distinct form of news consumption our participants engaged in on Facebook. It is their default mode for Facebook on both smartphone and laptop, described in terms of a desire or, more precisely, an urge to "keep it going," even when they are attracted to the content. Although participants found it difficult to verbalize what makes them want to limit their time with news items and why they keep on scrolling, other than the embodied urge "to keep it going," it appears that Facebook invites a sense of restlessness that encourages light, quick engagement with content, including the way it is navigated and physically handled with one move (a mouse scroll or a thumb scroll). For Ferdinand (30), even stopping or pausing was experienced as a disturbance:

> Should I click on the page? Because maybe there is something more interesting to read, but then I was just too impatient and I kept scrolling, I didn't want to stop.
>
> I thought [the video] was really nice but I don't wanna spend too much time doing it. This is the moment I remember thinking that I was like "ok, the information that I wanted is already [passed], so I can keep scrolling" but then I was like no maybe there is . . .

Getting out of the scrolling flow is laborious: one click can already be considered too much work. Julie (28) scrolled past a video that did not have subtitles: "If there'd been text at the bottom . . . I would've been more trig-gered to stay, you know, then I can consume the news without having to actually do ANOTHER action." Participants seem to not want to leave the flow of scrolling and feel they must get back to their feed as soon as possible when they do get out of it.

Participants seemed to have ambivalent feelings toward the practice of scrolling. On the one hand, they referred to it as a mindless activity that is something of a waste of time. Sarah (23): "Once you start doing it, you never get out of it. . . . Then [later] you see how far down you went and you're like 'Wow yeah, what did I actually see?'" On the other hand, this mindlessness is exactly what makes the practice an appealing break from serious activities like working and studying. Sarah explains: "[During] those moments . . . you don't really have to make a choice . . . because you only choose to go to that site [Facebook] and then you don't have to do anything but keep scrolling."

Triangulation

In 2004, truth and trust were simply seen as basic characteristics of news. Since the introduction of social media, mis- and disinformation have affected different countries in different ways, but even in the Netherlands where trust in mainstream news remains relatively high (Newman et al., 2019; 2020), trust and truth are nowadays higher on our participants' agenda than they were in 2014. Consequently, contemporary news users are more concerned with verification practices we summarize as *triangulation*. In an academic context, triangulation is defined by Denzin (1978, p. 291) as "the combination of methodologies in the study of the same phenomenon."

The metaphor is derived from navigation that uses three reference points to locate an object's position. Triangulation in the context of news refers to the use of a variety of sources to verify the truth of a particular news story. Academics and journalists do it, but as we noted among our research participants, news users also make use of this verification method (cf. Costera Meijer, 2016).

Our research supports the existence of three different forms of triangulation. The first form is about gathering additional *evidence*. It takes place when users have doubts about the facticity of the news they consume and seek to verify the information through other sources (Tandoc et al., 2018; Wagner & Boczkowski, 2019). This happens when users want confirmation of a news story offered by a less trusted news source, such as Twitter, by checking other more reliable (typically mainstream) news sources. The second form is about gathering additional *details*. This includes checking Twitter and less reputable news sources that are quicker to update during developing news. For instance, Regina (26) refers to Dutch news site www. Telegraaf.nl as "fairly biased" but still visits them when she wants the very latest update on crime stories. Here speed takes precedence over accuracy. Users consult several sources in the hopes that one offers extra information which might be verified later on by a more reliable source.

These first and second forms of triangulation are also combined when during big events, users first consult social media to find information that has not yet been verified and later verify this information via official sources. During the 2015 terrorist attacks in Paris, Gregg (41), who had a cousin living there, first consulted Twitter when he heard about the attacks, because there was no information available yet on official news sites. Only afterward did he triangulate this information through mainstream news:

> NOS and Nu.nl didn't say anything . . . while Twitter was exploding . . . that there had been an attack and where it was and so on and so on. . . . And only 15 minutes later NOS and Nu.nl came. . . . Then I prefer staying on top of it [through Twitter]. . . . But then afterward [you go back to] NOS and Nu.nl, because they do have journalists, [to see] what really happened.

Edgerly et al. (2020) suggest a third motive to triangulate a story. They found that people "showed greater intent to verify when they encountered information from a source they considered credible or a headline they perceived to be congruent with their political identity, and thus perceived to be more truthful" (p. 65). This counterintuitive form of verification – you expect the news to be reliable – is understandable from the perspective that extra sources "provide fodder for arguments that a person's perspective is superior" and can be used to win future arguments (Edgerly et al., 2020, p. 66).

Avoiding and abstaining

While usually a distinction is made between those who intentionally and unintentionally avoid news (Van den Bulck, 2006; Skovsgaard & Andersen, 2020), as our focus is on what people do with news, we instead distinguish between intentionally *avoiding* and *abstaining* from news. We reserve the label *avoiding* for actively skipping or moving around news content due to its topic or valence. An example of topic-based avoidance is categorically skipping the sports section. Valence-based avoidance is about what Groot Kormelink (2020) has called "measured avoidance": "people's careful measuring of and slaloming around (negative) content to protect their frame of mind" (p. 9). This is illustrated by Julie (28), who consumes news regularly but avoids those topics that hit her too hard emotionally: "Everything I experience as negative I scroll through as quickly as possible, because I don't want to, I don't need to experience that" (see also Chapter 5).

Abstaining we reserve for the practice of deliberately staying away from or limiting one's exposure to news. An example of abstaining is provided by Joanne (32), who had recently decided to completely stop following the news. She explained that while before she consumed news for social reasons (i.e. to be able to join in conversation), she had now made the conscious decision not to care:

> the negativity of the news and that shit every single day, every single day, and I don't feel like it. So that's my own personal choice, . . . I'm now to the point that I can think, "well, what other people think of that is their thing."

Joanne decided to stop checking the news not because she is uninterested in public affairs but because it made her feel uncomfortable. Letting go of the social obligation to keep up with the news was a relief. Abstaining from news resonates with Woodstock's (2014) notion of news resistance, used for those people who are "intentionally and significantly limiting their media use" (p. 837). While the concept of "avoiding" suggest a division between use and non-use, Woodstock (2014) describes resisting as a continuum. Indeed, we found that while very few participants deliberately abstain from all news, most occasionally feel the need to stay away from it. Another example of the latter form of abstaining comes from this book's authors: during the early weeks of the COVID-19 pandemic in 2020, they consciously tried to limit their consumption of news to a few times a day in an effort to relieve anxiousness (Tim) and to avoid distraction and disruption of one's concentration (Irene and Tim).

Linking, sharing, liking, recommending, commenting, voting, tagging

In 2014, we distinguished between several distinct social user practices that still exist five years later. First, there is a difference between sharing (clicking on a share or retweet button) and linking (copying and pasting the URL of a news article). Willem (30) explained that in the "rare case" he posts news on Facebook, he prefers "linking" to "sharing" for privacy reasons: "I don't really know exactly what happens when I 'share' on Facebook; I don't know how it gets shown and if there's other information that gets sent along." We also distinguished between liking (clicking on a like or heart button), recommending (clicking on "recommend"), commenting (leaving comments online), and voting (e.g. in response to a news poll, voting another user's post "up" or "down" on Reddit). The only practice we did not observe by 2019 is recommending, which seems to have disappeared alongside with the recommend button on Facebook. This illustrates how social user practices are also dependent on the specific affordances of the social media platforms (Van Dijck, 2013).

Since 2014, one new social user practice has become commonplace: tagging (Oeldorf-Hirsch & Sundar, 2015). This refers to the practice of tagging another user in the comment section underneath a social media post. These tags are often not accompanied by any text or only with an emoticon. This is a phatic form of communication that Miller (2008; see also Duffy & Ling, 2020) describes as follows:

> although they may not always be "meaningless," they are almost always content-less in any substantive sense. The overall result is that in phatic media culture, content is not king, but "keeping in touch" is. More important than anything said, it is the connection to the other that becomes significant, and the exchange of words becomes superfluous.
>
> (p. 395)

Although these seven social user practices are distinct, what is similar are the considerations concerning whether or not to engage in these practices. As Regina (26) indicated, she does not usually share, like, or comment on news on Facebook because she "does not want to present herself too much on social media." In this context, Picone (2011) argued that what keeps users from liking, sharing, or reacting to a news story is not so much the difficulty of writing a comment but the anticipated response of other users to it. This explains Regina's reluctance to express herself on social media. When she does "like" a news article, she is mindful of the impression she makes: "Then I'm pretty aware of what is in the article and what other people might think of me because of that." Taking care of one's self-image, then, is an important consideration in deciding whether or not to engage in social media. Kevin (26) refers to his public on Facebook as "all and sundry," suggesting he finds news too private an affair to discuss out in the open. This reasoning may also explain the recent shift of sharing and discussing news to more private social platforms such as WhatsApp (Newman et al., 2019; Swart et al., 2018).

Clustering the practices

Although each of the 24 practices has its unique internal logic, it is also possible to cluster them. However, these clusters are not mutually exclusive; no one grouping can do justice to the richness of the distinct practices. We identify several key dimensions along which the practices overlap, including function, intensity, intentness, efficiency, urgency, rhythm, and pleasure. First, *reading, watching*, and *listening* are about in-depth understanding and intense pleasure: intendedly taking a moment to really immerse yourself in the subject at hand. *Hearing* and *viewing* are lean-back practices that are more about enjoying an atmosphere and setting the mood rather than about focusing intently on content. *Glancing, snacking*, and *scrolling* are about being laid-back in the sense of getting an impression of what's going on without really engaging. They are also about diversion, taking a break from serious activities. *Checking, scanning*, and *monitoring* are characterized by a sense of urgency. They are not about understanding but about *knowing* that something happened (or not): staying on top of things and getting the gist of what's going on. *Saving* is a combination of being laid-back and intent: it is about delaying your engagement with a particular story. *Searching* and *triangulating* are intense practices focused on finding a reliable answer to a specific topic of interest. *Avoiding* and *abstaining* are characterized by intentness: they involve an ongoing effort to stay away from specific content or news altogether. Finally, *clicking* is the most multidimensional practice because it can fulfill (or lead to) a wide variety of functions, from deeply delving into a topic to entertaining oneself with silly content (see Chapter 3).

We propose calling the social media practices linking, sharing, liking, recommending, commenting, voting, and tagging "small acts of communication" instead of "small acts of engagement" (Picone et al., 2019). From a user perspective, these practices make more sense as communication gestures. These small acts are usually meant to communicate something to others rather than having the intention to "engage with the product," which makes more sense from a production angle. Small acts of communication exist on a spectrum from smaller to minuscule acts of communication and from content-related acts (engaging with news itself) to phatic acts of communication. Phatic acts of communication are only about communication and keeping in touch (Duffy & Ling, 2020; Miller, 2008). On the spectrum from phatic to content, tagging is on the left (phatic), whereas voting and commenting are on the right (content). Liking, recommending, linking, and sharing are in between, as they can be both phatic and content driven. The act of sharing, for instance, is phatic if you share news (e.g. via screenshot) just to let someone know you are thinking about them and content related if you share news you care about or you expect the other to be interested in.

Conclusions

In this chapter, we undertook a synthesizing qualitative analysis of different audience studies conducted between 2004 and 2020 to gain a better understanding of people's changing news consumption and to broaden and deepen the existing professional and academic vocabulary about news use. What people actually do with news and how they themselves experience and name this turns out to be substantially more varied than is often assumed. We distinguish between 24 user practices that differ in function, impact, intensity, efficiency, focus, and rhythm: reading, watching, viewing, glancing, listening, hearing, checking, snacking, scanning, monitoring, searching, clicking, saving, scrolling, triangulating, avoiding, abstaining, linking, sharing, liking, recommending, commenting, voting, and tagging.

A first conclusion is that the popular assertion that digital, social, and mobile media have unleashed an all-out revolution in the way people deal with news is both true and untrue. There *have* been fundamental changes, because digital innovations like smartphones and news apps have lowered the threshold to news consumption. In 2004–2005, there was a major concern about declining news use among people under 40 (Costera Meijer, 2006, 2007; Mindich, 2005). Illustrative for this group is Mark (29), who never paid attention to news until he got a smartphone in 2011. Using news became so easy (and even entertaining) that checking a news app was the first thing he did when he woke up. In 2020 this news app is still part of his checking cycle. Second, the digitalization of journalism has deepened, diversified, and increased the opportunities and options for using news. For instance, *reading* is not confined to newspapers or magazines but is also used on computers, tablets, and smartphones. *Checking* may go hand in hand with smartphone use but is also tied to newspapers and even television. *Triangulation* as a form of comparing and contrasting sources of news in order to get a broader, more truthful picture may occur between news sites but also involve TV, radio, or newspapers.

Second, (new) news user practices increasingly influence other social and cultural practices as well as the experience of the time and environment in which they occur. If in 2004–2005, having a TV dinner, checking a news site at work, or reading the newspaper over breakfast were experienced as intertwined yet separate activities, today news usage seems hardly separable from other practices: no one will find it odd anymore when people do a "checking cycle" in bed after they turn off the alarm or during social experiences like having a drink or grabbing a bite. This coincides with a certain intensification of the experience of time: if in 2004–2005 people read (free) dailies in the bus or train to work to fight boredom, ten years later the checking cycle even fills micro-moments of waiting for the red light or elevator (cf. Chapter 4).

Third, the checking cycle illustrates the broadening definition of what counts as news to users: not just events as described by journalists but everything that is new: from the developments in the personal life of your Facebook friends and opinions on Twitter to information on specific websites within your field. Conquering a spot for themselves in this checking cycle has become an important challenge for news media. Particularly, the "smartphone lockscreen" has become, as Newman (2016) argues, "a critical battleground for publishers, platforms and advertisers" (p. 7), fighting for the user's attention with push notifications.

Fourth, contrary to the distinctions between particular demographic *groups*, target groups, or types of *users* suggested by news repertoire analysis (Hasebrink & Popp, 2006), our comparative research points to distinctive news user *practices* which are not automatically linked to groups or user types. News wants and needs, place, moment of the day, and especially the convenience of a particular news carrier device appear to be defining factors in what people do with news. As Regina (26) explained, she *checks* the news on her smartphone and her work computer during the day, *snacks* the news on her laptop and in the newspaper after work, and *reads* her newspaper's weekend supplements on Saturday morning at home.

Although Schrøder and Larsen (2010) already found that the same news medium can be used for both overview and depth, this dichotomy may do too little justice to the variety of practices related to news. For instance, checking may seem to be about overview, but the checking cycle is more specifically about the need to quickly be on top of things, not just news but also developments in the lives of friends and acquaintances or within one's field of work. Clicking can result from a need for more depth but is often done out of curiosity or a need for a conversation topic.

Fifth, if technology has always served as an actor in its own right, this dimension has grown stronger in recent years (Domingo, Masip, & Costera

Meijer, 2015). A TV set, radio, or computer has to be turned on, but a push message on a smartphone or tablet acts on its own accord: it produces a bleep or buzz when something important has happened. This alert tends to make people drop whatever activity they were engaged in. Similarly, the sound of an incoming e-mail, app, text message, or Facebook notification lures people to their smartphone, tablet, laptop, or computer, tempting many to do another quick "checking cycle" to see what else is new.

Sixth, recent fears (and narratives) about fake news seem to have made the triangulation of news a more common concern (Wagner & Boczkowski, 2019). When users doubt the veracity of the news or the source, they check other, more trusted news sources, just like professionals do when they want to check the accuracy of information.

Seventh, unlike often assumed, the interests of news users may not be captured in clicks. For instance, checking, snacking, and scanning do not necessitate a click, and scrolling is even an explicit anti-clicking form of news use. This means that journalists and journalism scholars would do well to be cautious with taking clicking metrics as a standard for the level of interest or importance attached to a news item. In other words, to click or not to click does not automatically point to a news gap (Boczkowski & Mitchelstein, 2013), nor to a need to alter the selection of news (Stromback, Djerf-Pierre, & Shehata, 2012; Nieuwsmonitor, 2013). We further address this point in Chapter 3.

Eighth, in a world oversaturated with news, (actively) abstaining and avoiding news are practices almost everyone engages in sometimes. While news avoidance is overwhelmingly seen as a threat to the vitality of democracy, Woodstock (2014, p. 834) argues that intentional news resisters emphasize "the benefits of limited news consumption – greater calm and purpose, a constructive attitude toward the present and future, a willingness to work with others – qualities that enable news resisters to engage in meaningful political participation." And vice versa, many people who consume lots of political news, as Hersh (2020) argues, are "political hobbyists" and "motivated by their emotional needs and a pursuit of personal gratification rather than a deeper commitment to the common good" (Hersh, 2020, p. 10).

Finally, our results suggest that news is not necessarily becoming a *more* social experience. First, people still tend to share their news the way they did 15 years ago, offline (on the street, at the water cooler) and during particular moments (start of the workday, while walking the dog, etc.), where people are looking for a conversation topic. If sharing news via WhatsApp is easier and more efficient than waiting until you actually come across your neighbors, that does not make digital sharing automatically more "social." Second, our analysis gives little reason to believe that people en masse want to actively engage with news through linking, commenting, and so forth.

In 2014, we already signaled that these "small acts of communication" are characterized by concerns about personal reputation and privacy: what and to whom do I communicate about myself by engaging in these practices? It is therefore not surprising that they are shifting more toward private platforms (Newman et al., 2019; Swart et al., 2018).

Note

1 Revised and fully updated version of Costera Meijer, I., and Groot Kormelink, T. (2015). Checking, sharing, clicking and linking: Changing patterns of news use between 2004 and 2014. Originally published in *Digital Journalism*, *3*(5), 664–679.

3 What clicking actually means[1]

In the previous chapter, we introduced "clicking" as a distinct user practice. Here this practice is explored further. We argued in Chapter 1 that both scholars and news professionals have tended to take clicks at face value by assuming a close correspondence between clicking behavior and audience interests. Since "most-viewed lists" are often dominated by news about entertainment, crime, and sports, it is assumed that news users are more interested in "junk" than in "public affairs" news (politics, economics, international relationships) (e.g. Tenenboim & Cohen, 2015; Tewksbury, 2003). Boczkowski and Mitchelstein (2013) speak of a "news gap" between the preferences of journalists and news users. This chapter problematizes the relationship between clicks and audience interests. Instead of looking at clicks themselves, we observed how news users in everyday circumstances browse news and asked *them* what moves them to click or not to click. The aim of this chapter is to explore what clicking and not clicking mean to people and to what extent these practices reflect their news interests.

Professional autonomy versus pleasing the masses

Today, news organizations are able to minutely monitor the behavior of online news users. Through such tools as Chartbeat and Google Analytics, news professionals know exactly and often in real time how many users are spending how much time on which news item. Web metrics are not only monitored by individual journalists but also displayed on big screens in newsrooms and forwarded to staff by editors in chief. Monitoring audiences in itself is hardly new. Schlesinger (1978, p. 111) describes how the BBC News had a large wall chart tracking how its *Nine O'Clock News* was doing in the ratings. However, monitoring was done mostly to track how they were doing relative to their competitors. Contrary to today, the audience in itself was not an important consideration for journalists (Darnton, 1975; Gans, 1979; Schlesinger, 1978). Journalists had neither the tools nor the need for detailed knowledge about their audience, as one producer illustrates: "I know we have twenty million viewers, but I don't know who they are. I don't know what the audience wants, and I don't care" (Gans, 1979, p. 234). Indeed, journalists actively resisted audience feedback. In the early 2000s, public TV journalists interpreted any discussion of audiences as potentially compromising journalistic autonomy (Costera Meijer, 2003). Journalists also feared that taking audience preferences into consideration equaled lowering journalistic standards (Costera Meijer, 2013; Gans, 1979). This binary opposition between professional autonomy and pleasing the masses, between making quality journalism while users apparently prefer trivial news, is deeply ingrained in the journalism profession.

During the 2010s, however, journalistic considerations became more audience-centric. While ethnographic and interview-based studies show that journalists do continue to take their professional judgment and norma-tive ideals seriously (Karlsson & Clerwall, 2013; Nelson & Tandoc, 2018; Welbers, van Atteveldt, Kleinnijenhuis, Ruigrok, & Schaper, 2016), there has been an undeniable (if uneven) trend toward "measurable journalism" (Carlson, 2018). Research shows how, by and large, news organizations are having metrics like clicks inform their editorial decisions, from news presentation (news placement, headline adjustment) to news production (expanding or following up heavily clicked stories) (Anderson, 2011a; MacGregor, 2007; Vu, 2014). Cross-lagged analyses show that audience clicks affect both news placement (Lee et al., 2014) and subsequent report-ing (Welbers et al., 2016). Tandoc (2014) illustrates how editors select and deselect news items based on the web traffic they generate.

News organizations that aim for popularity (i.e. traffic) monitor clicks most closely, whereas those whose brand identity hinges on quality emphasize the importance of their professional judgment (Welbers et al., 2016). However, even public news organizations monitor clicks, justifying their use of pub-lic money by proving their ability to reach significant parts of the public (Hanusch, 2017; Karlsson & Clerwall, 2013). Journalists also monitor met-rics for personal validation: they want their stories to do well (Boesman & Costera Meijer, 2018; Cohen, 2019; Usher, 2013). Indeed, Christin (2014) found that even journalists with a critical attitude toward click-chasing do "understand online success as a signal of professional value" (n.p.). In recent years, as Cherubini and Nielsen (2016, p. 7) argue, skepticism toward clicks seems to have made way for "interest in how data and metrics can help newsrooms reach their target audiences and do better journalism."

Race to the bottom?

If journalism seems to be embracing metrics, scholars have generally looked at the impact of audience measurement on journalism with a critical eye (Carlson, 2018). Clicks in particular have been evaluated from a critical perspective, since clicking patterns are seen as evidence that users prefer junk news over news about public affairs (Boczkowski & Mitchelstein, 2013; Tenenboim & Cohen, 2015; Tewksbury, 2003). Clicks are typically measured in terms of the most read or viewed news stories, which are in turn used as a proxy for people's "preference" for or "interest" in news (e.g. Boczkowski & Mitchelstein, 2013; Schaudt & Carpenter, 2009; Tenenboim & Cohen, 2015). For instance, Schaudt and Carpenter (2009) conclude from most-viewed stories lists that readers "most preferred" the news values "proximity" and "conflict" and "least preferred" "timeliness" and "prominence." Similarly, Tenenboim and Cohen (2015) argue that "sensational topics and curiosity-arousing elements" being most heavily clicked indicates "that news consumers are mostly interested in non-public affairs news" (p. 212).

Such clicking patterns have led to concerns about the future of journalism and the subsequent implications for democratic societies. Although Nguyen (2013) notes that metrics "provide a considerable amount of accurate and reliable information for journalists and news executives . . . to serve people in a more considered, more scientific manner," he warns that using them uncritically can lead to "the dumbing down of news" and "a disaster for public life in the long term" (p. 157). Tandoc and Thomas (2015) argue that the use of metrics "has the potential to lock journalism into a race towards the lowest common denominator, ghettoizing citizens into bundles based on narrow preferences and predilections rather than drawing them into a community" (p. 247). Indeed, if clicking patterns were to lead journalists to produce more junk news in an effort to attract more eyeballs, this could lead to "a race to the bottom" (Nguyen, 2013).

However, user research suggests that clicking patterns may not accurately or fully capture the interests or preferences of news users. In Chapter 2, we described how people engage in several digital user practices that do not necessitate clicks, such as "checking," "monitoring," "scanning," and "snacking." In addition, illustrating how one's choice of metric is consequential, Von Krogh and Andersson (2016) found that measured in clicks (page views), "public sphere" accounted for 9% of online news consumption, whereas measured in spent time it made up 20%. These findings point to the "frequency fallacy": the misconception that what people use most frequently equates to what they find most important and what they use less frequently equates to what they find less important. This makes it crucial to understand what clicks actually mean. In this chapter, we therefore explore what it means when users click on news (interest?) and also what it means when they do not click (no interest?). Rather than looking at click-through rates to determine which headline characteristics entice users to click

(Kuiken, Schuth, Spitters, & Marx, 2017), we observed and asked what clicking and not clicking on news means to users *themselves*.

Methodology

To explore what clicks actually mean, we researched people's considerations for clicking and not clicking by looking at their everyday online news browsing. Our approach centered around the think-aloud protocol (cf. O'Brien, Freund, & Westman, 2014). First, participants were asked to describe how they use news throughout the day, focusing on the "multisensoriality" (Pink, 2009, p. 1) of their experiences (e.g. what they feel, taste, smell, hear, or see when using news). This approach allowed us to get a layered picture of their news use (e.g. checking news with an espresso or while riding the bus) and enabled our participants to call to mind their news user practices. Subsequently, using the concurrent think-aloud protocol (van den Haak et al., 2003), participants were instructed to browse news as they normally would – using their own devices and preferred websites and apps – and to say out loud all their steps and considerations. Participants were encouraged to comment on actions they failed to mention spontaneously. We argue that the subsequent loss of natural flow was warranted given our aim of uncovering considerations for (not) clicking; indeed, subtle or subconscious actions like scanning or scrolling past a headline were as important as consciously clicking on news.

It should be noted that although most participants had little problem verbalizing their motivations, news users may not know precisely what they want and why they want it. Yet, we argue that having participants provide their own account of why they did (not) click might give a more accurate reflection of what clicking means to them than having them choose from pre-selected categories, as is often the case in uses and gratifications research (for an overview, see Ruggiero, 2000). Although socially desirable answers should never be ruled out, the ease with which participants "admitted" to reading entertainment or being tired of news about Syria suggests we obtained a fair picture of the news they would normally (not) click. We also sought to limit social desirability by having the interviewers demonstrate the think-aloud protocol to participants using such "interviewer self-disclosures" (Lindlof, 1995, p. 182) as "I usually go to the entertainment section." Finally, participants were selected from the social network of the seven interviewers as "the development of a personal relationship" is crucial for interviews that go "deeply into the person's experiences" (Lindlof, 1995, p. 171).

We seek to map the whole spectrum of considerations for (not) clicking rather than look for the distribution, frequency, or representativeness of clicking patterns. Yet, common user patterns found across a relevant variety of news users might point to firmly anchored user patterns in general. A total of 56 people were interviewed in an everyday setting, typically their home. Participants were selected using "maximum variation sampling" which seeks to generate a wide range of data by including a broad spectrum of users (List, 2004). To enable capturing a variety of consideration for (not) clicking, our selection included 28 younger (aged 19–35) and 28 older (aged 50–65) users with various news habits (light or heavy digital use). The participants were from various (rural, urban) parts of the Netherlands, which at the time was already characterized by high rates of internet penetration (96%) and online news use (81%) (Newman, Fletcher, Levy, & Nielsen, 2016). We might, therefore, assume that their routines or preferences rather than obstructive technology (e.g. bad internet connection) were the main factors in the participants' browsing behavior. The interviews were conducted in February and March 2014 by seven journalism master's students from Vrije Universiteit Amsterdam and typically lasted 20–40 minutes. This included the browsing of websites and apps, which ranged from quick "checking cycles" (see Chapter 2) to lengthier reading sessions, depending on how the participant would normally use news. Devices used included computers, laptops, tablets, and smartphones. Visited websites and apps varied but often concerned major Dutch titles including www.NU.nl, www. NOS.nl, and www.Telegraaf.nl. The interviewers received extensive interview training and exhaustive feedback after each interview round. All interviews were recorded and transcribed. For the process of analysis we drew from the grounded theory method, using constant comparison between data and analysis and allowing categories to emerge from the data themselves (Corbin & Strauss, 1990).

Because we are interested in participants' own considerations for (not) clicking, the categories are illustrated through interview quotes. Even if some labels seem self-evident, exploring the meaning of clicks for users demands taking seriously the perspective of the participants. Also, participants often had multiple reasons for (not) clicking on one particular headline, but since we want to map the variety and range of their considerations, the quotes illustrate the categories in their "purest" form.

Considerations for clicking and not clicking

Following the procedures of the grounded theory method (Corbin & Strauss, 1990), we found 30 distinct considerations for clicking and not clicking. After an extensive process of axial coding, the first major distinguishing factor between the considerations appeared to be whether or not they were content-related. The content-related considerations proved to be further divisible into cognitive and affective considerations. Here, "cognitive" refers to considerations where the decision whether or not to click was made predominantly on a mental level ("thinking"), whereas "affective" refers to considerations where the decision was made predominantly on an emotional level ("feeling"). We use the term "predominantly" because the distinction between cognition and affect was more gradual than absolute. In the third category, participants' pragmatic considerations were their dominant reference point for clicking or not clicking, not their thoughts or feelings about content. For each consideration, we will note whether it concerns a reason to click or not to click (or both). Where applicable, we will also discuss how the considerations relate to selection criteria of news professionals (cf. O'Neill & Harcup, 2009), as our participants sometimes interpreted "news values" slightly differently.

Cognitive considerations

Recency and importance might be expected to be dominant considerations from a production perspective (cf. Golding & Elliott, 1979), yet were not mentioned much by our participants. *Recency* refers to whether the participant sees the news as timely or current. The limited mentions of this consideration seem to contradict research that indicates how users anticipate being presented with the latest news online (Bergström, 2008; Groot Kormelink & Costera Meijer, 2014). However, we argue that from a user perspective, recency may constitute a general prerequisite for online news but not an important consideration when deciding which particular news item to *click* on.

Importance refers to whether the participant views the news as significant in the conventional sense. However, if from a professional perspective importance is about "need to know" (Golding & Elliott, 1979, p. 118), from a user perspective "ought to know" is a more accurate description. Sandra (25) illustrates how the placement of news on a website influences how important she perceives it to be:

> "Cabinet: no clear picture of money laundering," I couldn't care less, so wouldn't click on that. . . . If it was REALLY important it would have been big at the top [of the homepage]. Then maybe I would've clicked on it.

Online news presented as important through prominent placement on the website or news app is experienced as more worthy of knowing; if the same news is placed less prominently, it apparently is not significant enough to deserve a click. Like recency, importance is not a dominant consideration when deciding which individual headline to click on. They are not so much selection criteria for (not) clicking on news as prerequisites for selecting a news site or app in the first place. Indeed, reflecting the original function of the front page of newspapers, users do expect (professional) news websites or apps to show them what is recent and important (Groot Kormelink & Costera Meijer, 2014).

Participants often clicked on news that had *personal relevance*, relating to their everyday life, including work. This consideration is dual, meaning that it counts as reason to click when present and as reason not to click when absent. Henry (55), who invests, clicked on a news item about the stock market but skipped a headline concerning the shares of a specific company: "I [don't invest] in companies, so the particular company mentioned here I couldn't care less about." Matthew (25) clicked on a headline about the Samsung Galaxy S5 "because I want to buy a new phone" but skipped news about rental housing because "after [I leave my student house] I'm not going to rent, I will buy something immediately."

Golding and Elliott (1979) distinguish between the professional selection criteria *geographical proximity and cultural proximity*, and from a user perspective we found a similar distinction. Both considerations are dual. First, participants tended to click if they saw the headline as concerning news taking place within their immediate surroundings, regardless of absolute distance. Bianca (54) clicked on a headline about a dead body found 20 km away from her hometown: "[City] is so close, I just wanna know. . . . And if it's not so close then it's not interesting." Yet Tracy (53) skipped a headline about an accident that happened within a similar distance because she did not experience it as nearby: "I think it didn't happen in this region but somewhere in the south. No, that doesn't really interest me." Golding and Elliot's (1979) "cultural proximity" depends "on what is familiar and within the experience of journalists and their audience," but for our participants, more specifically, it refers to whether they recognize a kinship with the subject of the news, again regardless of absolute distance (p. 166). Leonard (24) clicked on sports news concerning compatriots: "I like cycling, especially if Dutch people are participating. . . . I don't have to know if some Slovak won a round in Poland." Conversely, Andrew (58) did not click on a headline regarding Antilleans in the Netherlands because he does not feel a connection: "It may be important, but . . . not for me right now. . . . Because I don't do anything with Antilleans. . . . I mean, I don't know one Antillean and I don't know if they're good or bad."

Whereas for journalists *unexpected* refers to rare, out-of-the-ordinary developments (Galtung & Ruge, 1965), from a user perspective it is about whether the news fits *their* idea of what is common. Lilly (26) clicked on a headline about a joint action from a trade union and an employers' organization: "Seems interesting, I'm curious why [they] are on the same page here, seems a bit illogical." It is important to stress that what is unexpected to journalists may not be experienced as unexpected by users, and vice versa. For instance, Anita (21) did not click on news about a man setting himself on fire: "Yeah, it's bad, but it's, I don't care . . . because uhm, yeah it happens regularly."

Related to "unexpected" is the reason *this is logical*, where the user does not click because from their perspective the news is (too) obvious. Regarding the headline "Nokia unsure about brand name for the future," Nanda (21) noted that she already knew Nokia was not doing well: "Then this seems like a logical continuation. Then I don't have to read it, because I already know why that is."

Like journalists selecting stories already in the news (Galtung & Ruge, 1965; Harcup & O'Neill, 2001), participants regularly clicked on *follow-ups* to stories they had read before. Lauren (26) illustrates, "What catches my eye immediately is the headline. . . . 'Exam fraud [school] costs 3 million euro.' I've followed [that story] before." A dominant reason not to click was that the participant *already knew* about the news. Not to be confused with "follow-up," where users click on a new development, here they are already familiar with this particular development, as Karen (50) indicates: "[This] I already just heard, so I'm not going to read that again."

A dominant dual consideration was whether the subject of the headline *rang a bell* with the participant. This concerned famous people but also names or events the participants recognized but could not quite place, as Nina (54) illustrates: "That Benno L., you've heard something about that before and then [you're] like, gosh, who was that Benno L. again?" Conversely, Eddy (53) asks why he would click if the subject matter does not ring a bell: " 'Fight parenting clinic and insurer resolved,' well, I wouldn't know what a parenting clinic is, so [laughs] I'm like, why should I read that?"

More detail on particulars comes into consideration when the headline raises a specific question in the participant's mind, causing them to want to know more about the situation, as Jack (56) illustrates: "Heavy weather in Italy, I see. . . . [clicks] What is going on here?" For a similar reason, Karen (50) clicked on a headline about a fishing ban: "Then I'm like, what do we catch there? . . . What kind of fish is swimming there?"

Another reason to click was that the news enables participants to *join in conversation*. Rod (24) explains why he clicked on a headline about the Winter Olympics:

> Because if you start a conversation with people then often you want to talk about things that uh are recent and speak to a lot of people and uh

the Winter Olympics I think are a part of that, so uhm to be able to join in the conversation, so to speak.

Rod's reason for clicking is the social utility function the topic provides: fodder for conversation. Teacher Joe (26) similarly clicked on a headline about the "'largest lunar impact ever recorded' because I also talk about that with my students."

Participants also clicked if they had *their own opinion* about a headline and wanted to see how it was discussed in the article. Jenna (27) clicked on the headline "World Bank freezes aid to Uganda over gay law" because "I personally have an opinion about it, so I'm curious on what grounds the World Bank does something like that." However, this consideration was uncommon; like in Donsbach's (1991) study that relativized the influence of cognitive dissonance on readers' selections, our participants rarely expressed strong opinions about headlines. If they did, disagreement was not a reason *not* to click.

Participants regularly did not click on news they thought was repeating itself. We labeled this *supersaturation*. Bruce (55) noted about the ongoing crisis in Syria: "Because every day it's the same, same, same, at some point it becomes less interesting. Even though it's not less terrible." Though similar to "compassion fatigue" (Moeller, 1999), supersaturation is more about how hearing about it *again* does not provide new insights. The headline does not invite a click anymore, as Jeff (58) illustrates: "You actually drown in that kind of news. At some point you're like, it's not going to stop anyway. It's not that it's not important, but *it doesn't stop.*" As we will elaborate later, not wanting to click on a headline does not mean the user does not want to *see* it. But for now the headline itself provides a sufficient update about the situation; it is not until "something completely new" happens that Jeff (58) will click again.

Some participants clicked on headlines that offered a *new perspective.* This is not about the news event being unexpected but about the headline offering "the other side" of a topic. Such news inspires because it adds to your knowledge or broadens your horizon and as such functions as an eye-opener (cf. Costera Meijer, 2013). Corbin (24) illustrates:

> Here's an article called "According to these three imams the Koran has nothing against gays." That's interesting to me [because] you have this image that in the Koran it says that homosexuality is wrong and here it says something completely different, and I'm curious how that is substantiated by those imams.

Rather than the topic of homosexuality and Islam, it is the original angle of the headline that makes Corbin click.

Sometimes, participants clicked on a headline because they wanted to see for themselves or "experience" what happened. We labeled this *participatory perspective*. An example is Nick (24), who clicked on the headline "Man makes illegal base jump from moving ski lift" because he "can't really picture how anyone would do that" and hoped to see it in a video.

A reason not to click was that the headline was *just an opinion*. Regarding a developing story about the possible resignation of a minister, Tara (20) noted, "If a decision really has been taken, I'll find it interesting, but . . . nine out of ten times it's blether. . . . If [prime minister] says '[He] is staying,' then that's not a truth but just an opinion." What keeps Tara from clicking is the lack of validity or decisiveness.

A similar reason for not clicking was *disjointed news fact*, where the participant does not want to read a story until it is finalized. Tara is not interested in clicking on isolated updates about developments she is already aware of: "I don't need to have that information in between, . . . I want the *answer*, you know, the *conclusion*." From a user perspective, even the conclusion of a story can be a disjointed news fact. Mark (52) did not click on a headline concerning a resolved conflict, because he was not aware of the problem in the first place: "You have to know what the problem is [and] then you can also know: what is the solution? . . . But yeah, just an isolated little fact, I would never read that." About a headline regarding the conflict in Ukraine, he similarly argued that it concerned a detail too small to warrant a click. If he were to click, he would also want to know the context: "What is the cause? How did it happen? What happened? Why do they do it? What do they want to achieve?" This suggests that Mark would appreciate a headline like "Five things you should know about the crisis in the Ukraine" that allowed him to get a full picture of the situation within one article.

An important finding was that sometimes the participant did show (signs of) interest in particular news items and yet did not click. The narrative construction of the headline appeared to be a relevant factor. A frequent occurrence was that the participants showed interest in the news itself but the headline was *informationally complete* and consequently, they did not expect to be better informed by clicking. Lauren (26) noted, " 'More than 4 million viewers for Olympic finals 1500 meters,' that's a fun fact to know, but I know that this is usually all the information you're gonna get, so I don't really have to click it anymore." This is the opposite of clickbait: Lauren is interested in the topic, but there is no need to click because the headline tells the whole story. Nick (24) similarly illustrates, "I see it says 'Final will be great,' so I already know they're in the final so I don't necessarily have to click it."

Finally, sometimes there was an *associative gap*: despite the participants' apparent interest in a topic, the headline did not tell them enough to want to click. Ella (51) read, "Pieterburen [location of a famous seal sanctuary] will possibly move to [island]" and said, "The headline doesn't tell me much, that's why I don't click it." However, later in the interview she did click on a headline that explicitly mentioned "seals" and said she was fascinated by them. Clearly, she had not made the connection between Pieterburen and seals. Based on clicks, it would be tempting to conclude that Ellen was not interested in this article, but based on her comments about how much seals "intrigue" her, it seems safe to assume that she is. Similarly, Matthew (25) was clear about his interest in clicking the headline "Warning Kerry about Cold War Ukraine," claiming he was following all news about the country because he planned to visit the city of Chernobyl, "and of course I'm not gonna go there if there is almost a civil war." Yet, he did not click on a headline about former Ukrainian president Yanukovych because "I don't know exactly who that is, so I think I would skip that." While this consideration is similar to "ring a bell," the focus here is not the topic; instead, it is about not being able to make a connection between the headline and the user's (pre-existing) interest in the topic.

Cognitive considerations

* *Recency*. Whether the user sees the news as timely or current.
* *Importance*. Whether the user sees the news as something they ought to know.
* *Personal relevance*. Whether the topic has a relation to the user's everyday life.
* *Geographical proximity*. Whether the user sees the news as concerning their immediate surroundings.
* *Cultural proximity*. Whether the user recognizes a kinship with the news.
* *Unexpected*. Whether the user sees the news as surprising.
* *This is logical*. The user thinks the news is obvious.
* *Follow-up*. The user wants to know the sequel to a story they have been following.
* *Already know*. The user has already heard the news elsewhere.
* *Ring a bell*. Whether the protagonist or subject matter of the news rings a bell with the user.
* *More detail on particulars*. The user wants to know what exactly is going on.

- *Join in conversation.* The user expects to be able to bring the news up in conversation.
- *Own opinion.* The user wants to see how a topic they have an opinion about is discussed in the news.
- *Supersaturation.* The user thinks the news repeats itself too often.
- *New perspective.* The headline offers a different perspective that sheds new light on the topic.
- *Participatory perspective.* The user wants to witness the news event.
- *Just an opinion.* The user wants facts rather than opinions.
- *Disjointed news fact.* The user wants the whole story, not an isolated update.
- *Informational completeness.* The user has no need to click because the headline says it all.
- *Associative gap.* The user is unable to connect the headline to the topic.

Affective considerations

Participants clicked on *disheartening* headlines, similar to the news value "bad news" (Harcup & O'Neill, 2001). Sarah (21) illustrates, "This one I would read: 'Biker killed by car.' That's just sad." However, if participants found the headline too disheartening, they skipped it: "It's such a heavy text, 'Dragging patients is risky.' I prefer starting with happy news" (Jeff, 58). Indeed, on the other side of the emotional spectrum, participants clicked on lighthearted, fun headlines that made them *feel good*. Isabel (30) illustrates, "Something about self-cleaning plastic for cars. . . . Yeah, that's a fun news item. . . . It's light, . . . just nice to read." While this corresponds to the news value "good news" (Harcup & O'Neill, 2001), from a user perspective, "feel good" is about the impact of the news rather than its genre.

Similar to the news value Harcup and O'Neill (2001) labeled "entertainment," participants also regularly clicked on headlines that *bemused* them. More specific than wanting to be amused, they feel a strong urge to click on the headline because they feel excitedly puzzled by it. Eva (19) illustrates, "Something provocative like 'Anders Breivik: PlayStation 2 instead of PlayStation 3 is torture,' . . . then I think what is this about? And then I click it and read it." The colloquial term for this is clickbait – headlines with a "what-the-hell" factor that makes the user want to click, as Martin (24) illustrates: "Actually it never has any news value, but it's usually those headlines that make you think, yeah, I'm curious what it is exactly." Such headlines usually concern remarkable or bizarre news, which might partially explain why this type of news is so heavily clicked (cf. Tenenboim & Cohen, 2015). As we suggested in Chapter 2, clicking on these headlines is not about devoting your attention to news you care about; rather, it is about silly diversion, about clicking on something dumb for a laugh.

A reason not to click related to bemusement was that the participant felt the news was *bullshit*. Leonard (24) explains, "Now I see 'German cat survives 30-meter fall.' Then you're like, I don't care. . . . I think it's a bit rubbish actually." We classified this as affective instead of cognitive because it is a gut reaction dismissing the pettiness of the headline rather than a cognitive deliberation about whether or not the topic is nonsense. However, this consideration was mentioned less often than "bemusement," where the silliness of the headline was exactly what does make users click.

Another dominant dual consideration for (not) clicking was the *categorical welcome or rejection* of a particular "beat" or topic that participants felt enthusiasm or aversion toward, respectively. The latter was often the case with sports news, as Ruth (24) illustrates: "The last [headline] is sports news, sports mean nothing to me." Anita (21), on the contrary, categorically welcomes news about sports with which she has affinity but rejects others: "I don't find soccer interesting, so I skip those headlines automatically. But ice skating and tennis, those I do follow." While this consideration is similar to "personal relevance," the emphasis here is on the feeling the headline evokes rather than the recognition of how the topic relates to one's life.

Some participants clicked on headlines because they found the accompanying image *visually appealing*, also a selection criterion for journalists ("visual attractiveness") (Golding & Elliott, 1979, p. 155). Danny (25) is not interested in the news itself, but the picture evokes arousal: "Pretty often NU.nl has these stupid news items about, I don't know, a New Year's Day dive. Couldn't care less, but if it happens to have a picture of a lady, I do click on it."

A surprising finding was that some participants clicked on news that *gleefully annoyed* them. Lilly (26) clicked on the headline "President of Uganda will sign antigay law" because she found it "particularly bothersome that again there is a country that does not understand that homosexuality is not something you should draft a law against, so yeah, I'll read that news and be very irritated by it." Similarly, even though Isabel (30) was annoyed by a headline about a Dutch ice-skater who for competitive reasons chose to represent Belgium instead, clicked rather than ignored the item: "Now he thinks that the Netherlands should share their ice-skating knowledge. . . . It does evoke a bit of irritation, that headline. I'm like, *you* became Belgian."

Affective considerations

- *Disheartenment.* The user is saddened by the news.
- *Feel-good.* The lighthearted news makes the user feel good.
- *Bemusement.* The user feels excitedly puzzled by the headline.
- *Bullshit.* The user instantly dismisses of the pettiness of the headline.

- *Categorical welcome/rejection.* The user feels either enthusiasm or aversion toward the beat or the topic of the news.
- *Visual appeal.* The image evokes the urge to want to see more.
- *Gleeful annoyance.* The user is delightfully enraged by the news.

Pragmatic considerations

Some participants did not click on news that would *disrupt* an otherwise smooth user experience, for instance, due to loading time or commercials when clicking videos. Bruce (55) illustrates, "Then you have to sit through commercials before you can watch something. Well, I won't do that, I don't want to." A related reason not to click mostly associated with videos was that the item was *data-heavy*. Here platform specificity also plays a role. Joe (26) does click videos about wrestling news on his computer (Wi-Fi), but not on his smartphone (3G): "Videos . . . I'd rather not watch on my phone because, well, data heavy." Clicking would cost him too much.

Finally, participants did not click on news when it *did not fit their routine*. Josh (62) only has a few minutes to check headlines before he leaves for work, where the radio is playing the whole day. He skipped a headline about a poison gas attack in Syria, explaining, "That's very important, . . . but I'm sure I'll hear it on the radio." Similarly, Jenna (27) skipped a headline noting she would only click on it if she "really took the time to really dive into it." While interested, clicking right now did not fit her schedule.

Pragmatic considerations

- *Disruption.* Clicking will interrupt a smooth user experience.
- *Data-heaviness.* Clicking will use up too much data.
- *Does not fit routine.* Clicking does not match with the user's schedule.

Browsing patterns without click

Another important finding is that the participants engaged in online browsing patterns that did express interest in news, yet did not necessitate a click. We have previously labeled these distinct user practices "checking," "monitoring," "snacking," and "scanning" (Chapter 2). Checking means quickly and efficiently finding out whether anything new or interesting is happening by looking at the latest headlines. Clicks are not automatically involved, as Billy (52) illustrates: "For me it's important to just quickly see things, so just a [homepage] is fine, just the [headlines]. . . . I actually use it just to quickly see what the latest news is." Just because users do not click on an item does not mean that they do not want to see the headlines. Danny (25) explains, "It's nice that you kind of know what is happening in the world. Because let's say [the item] wasn't there anymore. . . . Then people start to talk and then you really don't know anything about it." For social purposes, then, he does want to check the latest important news: "The headlines I'd want, yes, but the articles themselves, uh, whatever."

Monitoring is actively surveying the informational environment to be able to come into action when necessary (see Chapter 2). Annabel (53) describes, "When those two criminals were on the loose last week, I constantly looked on my phone to see if they were caught. That was really scary." Even though Annabel was continually monitoring her smartphone for updates, no clicks were registered. In similar fashion, Henry (55) uses his phone to monitor his investments: "I return to that at least once every two hours, because I want to see how my portfolio is developing." In both the cases, their evident interest in news was not captured in clicks.

Snacking is defined as grabbing bits and pieces of information in a relaxed, easygoing fashion to gain a sense of what is going on (see Chapter 2). Danny (25) describes how he snacks on a website about movie news without clicking: "I scroll a bit and look at pictures and at movies and then I click away [from the site]."

Scanning means picking out the highlights of news in order to get the gist of the story (see Chapter 2). Tara (20) illustrates how scanning does not necessitate any clicking. Although she does want to know about the news, she scans words in the lead on the homepage to get the essence: "Like here: they 'foresee no profits,' it's about 'Dutch companies,' OK, then I know enough." As noted, even headlines can be so informationally complete that they do not necessitate a click even if the user is interested.

Conclusion and discussion

This chapter explored what clicking means from a user perspective and to what extent it reflects the interests of news users. Asking and observing how people browse online news, our findings point to the frequency fallacy: the news people click on most does not necessarily represent what they find most important, and what they click on least does not represent what they find least important. First, funny or remarkable headlines are clicked not because users truly value the content in question but because they want a laugh: it is a nice break from the serious headlines they see or the serious activities they are engaged in (work, studying). While this type of news may as a result be over-represented in "most-read" lists, our participants emphasize that this is not the only type of news they want to see; it is a fun, welcome supplement to being informed about important matters, even if the latter is just done through checking, scanning, or snacking headlines without clicking. Paradoxically, then, adhering to clicks by giving people more of what click numbers suggest they "want" might lead to the trivialization of news and *thus* to a decreasing interest of users. In a similar vein, ignoring how people appreciate checking, snacking, scanning, or monitoring headlines without the need to click on them underestimates how important these unclicked items can be for them.

Second, pragmatic considerations unrelated to interest in content (such as not wanting to interrupt a smooth user experience or "spend" data) interfere with users' clicking behavior. Third, headlines can tell users interested in particular topics too little (associative gap) to warrant a click. In other words, this was a missed opportunity that could have been prevented by a more informative headline. Fourth, headlines can also be informative enough (informational completeness) and therefore not require a click, because the user simply wants to know about (rather than understand) the news. If in 2014 the dominant example was the situation in Syria, in 2020 it was the COVID-19 pandemic: in the first couple of weeks they read a lot of news, but after some time *seeing* an update of the daily numbers of casualties was enough. Sophia (23) explains: "So I really do want to get updates and I find that very important and of course you get them every day, but I don't need to think about this every hour of the day so to speak, because life does go on." Confirming the frequency fallacy, the number of times she clicks on COVID-19 headlines does not correspond to the importance she attaches to it. Finally and relatedly, digital news user practices such as checking, monitoring, snacking, and scanning may not involve any clicking but do fulfill valuable functions for users, including being brought up to speed on the latest public affairs developments without interrupting one's flow. In terms of news interests, then, the news gap between news makers and news users may not be as wide or unbridgeable as Boczkowski and Mitchelstein (2013) suggest.

Illustrating the value of taking an explicit user-centered approach, we found 30 distinct considerations users have for clicking or not clicking, classifiable into three categories: cognitive, affective, and pragmatic. Rather than employing prefigured categories (e.g. from uses and gratifications theory), this approach resulted in a more complex account of people's digital news use. For instance, cognitive considerations are not limited to information seeking (surveillance) but include the (lack of) recognition of news (ring a bell, associative gap) and the perception of how news is presented (e.g. disjointed news fact, just an opinion, new perspective). Likewise, affective considerations go beyond entertainment or positive affect and include feelings of negative (disheartenment) and mixed affect (gleeful annoyance). Our user-centered approach has also generated a vocabulary for news values and selection criteria that puts focus not on how news is produced or presented but how it is received. The detailed labels might be relevant for journalism professionals seeking to understand what user experiences like enthusiasm and aversion are based on and provide a handle on how to effectuate or avoid such reactions.

Importantly, our argument is not that clicks are meaningless. Indeed, they can help news organizations to ensure that their audiences find the content they are interested in, through A/B testing of headlines or article placement (Cherubini & Nielsen, 2016). Although they have proved complex to monetize (Batsell, 2015; Cherubini & Nielsen, 2016), a combination of metrics that measure various forms of engagement (see Napoli, 2011) seems promising for gauging people's interests and preferences because they capture a broader array of digital user practices than only clicking. Such metrics could help organize websites and apps so as to accommodate users' diverse expectations and desires at different times and in different contexts. In addition, information about users might be used not for "ghettoizing citizens into bundles based on narrow preferences and predilections" (Tandoc & Thomas, 2015, p. 247) but for tracing and providing news that has "proportional relevance" (Costera Meijer, 2003) to different communities. For instance, students are not only interested in news about students but also (as participant Matthew suggested) interested in news about the starter-home market. However, each metric should be assessed critically rather than taken at face value. Our research has shown how an open, qualitative user-centered approach can help examine what metrics do and do *not* measure. We will further reflect on best practices for news organizations regarding metrics in Chapter 6.

If clicks only tell part of the story, our own methods are not without limitations either. The concurrent think-aloud protocol forces participants to consider and verbalize actions that in everyday life are often undertaken automatically or subconsciously. Therefore, we encourage other researchers to further explore clicking and not clicking using different methods, such as (video-)ethnography (see Chapter 5), tracking devices, or screen capture tools.

Finally, Harambam, Helberger, and van Hoboken (2018) suggest an alternative recommender system which does not use clicks as input for algorithmic news recommenders (ANR) but instead gives people agency to adjust recommendations according to their interests and wishes as an expression of "voice." One of their proposals is to develop algorithmic recommender types, not only as an alternative to clicks as input for recommendations but also as alternative to news reader types. The choice is not what kind of news people need or supposedly want but "from what kind of recommender persona they would like to receive recommendations" (Harambam et al., 2018, p. 15). As examples, they suggest five algorithmic recommender personae:

"the Explorer (news from unexplored territory), the Diplomat (news from the other side), the Wizard (surprising news), the Moral Vacationer (guilty pleasures), or the Expert (specialized news based on previous consumption)" (Harambam et al., 2018, p. 14).

Note

1 This chapter is a revised and updated version of Groot Kormelink, T., and Costera Meijer, I. (2018). What clicks actually mean: Exploring digital news user practices. Originally published in *Journalism*, *19*(5), 668–683.

4 A user perspective on time spent

Temporal experiences of everyday news use[1]

"Four out of ten Dutch people barely read or watch news." This rather alarmist headline was published by Dutch newspapers (Obbink, 2017; Het Parool, 2017) after the Netherlands Institute for Social Research released their 2017 report "Dutch people and news." The headline was likely based on the following excerpt from the report's press release:

> More than half of the population (61%) on an average day uses at least one news medium and spends at least five consecutive minutes on using news media.
>
> (SCP.nl, 2017)

In the research report, its authors provided more nuance: when also including news use with a duration of fewer than five consecutive minutes, the percentage of Dutch people who consume news every day went from 61 to 79 (and on a weekly basis even to 95) (Wennekers & de Haan, 2017, p. 8).

This anecdote is illustrative of a trend in journalism and its study: to measure news consumption in terms of how much time people spend on it. Recognizing the limits of clicks, both in the newsroom (e.g. Cherubini & Nielsen, 2016; Cohen, 2019) and within journalism studies (Molyneux, 2018; Nelson & Lei, 2018; Thurman, 2018; Thurman & Fletcher, 2019), "time spent" is used to measure the consumption of news items, platforms, or brands. As any researcher will quickly point out, time spent (like any metric) is not a neutral measure of news consumption; one's choice of metric always impacts the results. This, again, is illustrated by Swedish research comparing news use measured both through page views (clicks) and time spent: in page views, "public sphere" news accounted for 9%, whereas measured in time spent, it accounted for 20% (von Krogh & Andersson, 2016). Likewise, studying online news audiences, Nelson and Webster (2016) found no correlation between size (unique visitors) and engagement (time spent). Still, time spent has been recognized as a viable metric for audience attention because it allows for comparisons across platforms (Thurman, 2018). Since time spent is likely to remain a dominant measure of news consumption, it is worthwhile to further explore what exactly it does and does not measure.

In Chapter 1 we introduced the "duration fallacy," the misconception that the time people spend on news signals what they find most important or interesting. This fallacy has two components. The first is the assumption that one can use "time spent" to make inferences about news users' interests or preferences. Keeping with the Swedish example, it is easy to see how the page view numbers may be used to support claims about the public's appetite for "junk news," whereas the time spent results may serve as evidence of their interest in public affairs news. Potentially problematic about basing audience understanding (solely) on metrics is that these are not intended to capture the interests or experiences of news users but are rather a measure designed by the news industry, ultimately to quantify and sell users' attention to advertisers (Ang, 1991; Napoli, 2011; Webster, 2014). What follows is that "problems" and "solutions" regarding news use also tend to be framed in ways beneficial to this industry (cf. Keightley & Downey, 2018). For example, in the "attention economy" (Davenport & Beck, 2001), which sees news media competing for the finite resource that is the audience's attention, measuring news use in terms of time spent quickly leads to the question of how the time people spend on news can be increased. An alternative starting point is the perspective of the news users, which instead raises such questions as how and why people engage in short news practices like "checking" and "scanning" (Chapter 2) and how they might be better served both informationally and experientially.

The second component of the duration fallacy is the assumption that more time spent on news use is inherently or automatically desirable. What the aforementioned exclusion of short news sessions implies is that practices like "checking" or "scanning" are less legitimate or desirable forms of news use. This may at first sight seem understandable for news organizations which interpret more attention minutes as equal to more revenue or better public service. However, as we will show in this chapter, more time spent does not necessarily reflect a better public service, nor is maximizing time spent necessarily the best route for building a durable relationship with your audience. From a societal standpoint, following the notion of an informed citizenry, it is also generally taken for granted that users spending more time on news is beneficial. However, while it may seem reasonable to qualify people who indicate spending "no time at all" on (traditional) news as "disconnected citizens" (Blekesaune et al., 2012), it is quite another question whether *more* time spent on news necessarily translates into being *more* engaged; that is, whether the relationship between spending time on news and being an engaged citizen is linear. A related question is whether there is a threshold in terms of time news use that must be crossed in order to count as legitimate news use.

The aim of this chapter is to add to and deepen existing research on time spent and news consumption by exploring what spending time on news means from an explicit user perspective. It does so by drawing upon three qualitative user studies that center around the notion of experience.

Literature: time and news use

Central as time is to journalism, it has received limited explicit attention in journalism studies (Bødker & Sonnevend, 2018; Zelizer, 2018). The same is true for research on news use: although time is featured frequently, it is rarely problematized. Time is typically approached in roughly one of three ways. In the first approach, time serves as the *unit of analysis*. The constructs used most often for measuring news consumption are frequency and duration (time spent). Frequency refers to the times per day, week, or month news is used and is typically measured through surveys (e.g. Molyneux, 2018; Stromback et al., 2013). Duration as expressed in minutes spent on news use is typically measured via tools like Google Analytics (von Krogh & Andersson, 2016) and comScore (Nelson & Lei, 2018), surveys (Aalberg, Blekesaune, & Elvestad, 2013; Blekesaune et al., 2012; Molyneux, 2018), or a combination thereof (Thurman, 2018; Thurman & Fletcher, 2019). A benefit of minutely measuring time spent is that it allows for detailed and precise comparisons between different news media, platforms, brands, or genres. This has led to valuable insights, such as Nelson and Lei's (2018) finding that mobile app users spend significantly more time on news than those who use a mobile browser, and Thurman and Fletcher's (2019) finding that the impact of the digital distribution of news on how much time people spend on news differs per age group and per newspaper brand.

In the second approach, time is seen in terms of the *temporal organization* of news use, often in relation to spatial and social dimensions (Peters, 2016; Silverstone, 1994). Methods include diaries (e.g. Courtois et al., 2013; Dimmick et al., 2011; Hoplamazian et al., 2018) and/or (digital) logs (Van Damme et al., 2015). The focus here is typically on how news use is dispersed throughout people's day or week and/or how it is embedded within other activities. For instance, Dimmick et al. (2011) found that mobile news occupies a new spatiotemporal niche they call "interstices," defined as "the gaps in the *routines* of media users *between scheduled* activities" (23, emphasis added).

In the third approach, the focus is on the *temporal characteristics of the news* itself, most commonly in terms of speed. Subsequently, these characteristics are used either for inferring about news use or as input for research into news use. In the first variant, people's experience or engagement with news is read off news production logics; Keightley and Downey (2018) summarize that it is often assumed that

> speedily produced news content and fast, flexible technologies of delivery will necessarily produce temporal experiences which are characterized predominantly by speed and, in many cases, that this will routinely produce superficial engagement with the news, or alienation from it altogether.
>
> (p. 105)

Spending less time with news is thus equated with staying on the surface and being less interested (or even uninterested) in news. Conversely, Slow Journalism (a critical response to the negative effects associated with speed in journalism practice) is linked to such notions as "responsible citizenship" (Le Masurier, 2015, p. 149). In the second variant, the temporal characteristics of the news are used as input for research on news use. For instance, based on features distilled from academic literature, Drok and Hermans (2016) surveyed users' interest in Slow Journalism using such items as preferences for in-depth reporting and explanation. Similar examples include research surveying news users' preferences for characteristics of online news (production), such as continuous updates (Bergström, 2008) and immediacy of reporting (Van der Wurff & Schoenbach, 2014).

More recently, two articles on news use have engaged critically with the notion of time itself. Peters and Schrøder (2018) argue that research has tended to focus on the "here and now" and make the case for a process-based approach to studying news repertoires that focuses on "the emergence, maintenance, and (re)formation of audiences' news repertoires in everyday life and across the lifespan" (p. 1079). Keightley and Downey (2018) instead have explored how people themselves experience and navigate the temporal logics surrounding their news use. This aligns with Zelizer's (2018) critique of how time is typically seen as a "blank slate," taking "shape more *in response to* complex settings than as a result of other kinds of interactions" (113). Using the notion of "zones of intermediacy" (Keightley, 2013), Keightley and Downey (2018, p. 100) focus on "the experiential arenas in which temporal meaning is produced at the juncture of times – embodied, social, cultural, historical and technological." This concept draws attention to (1) how temporal experiences are produced where several temporalities meet (e.g. clock time, work time) and (2) how the temporalities of news texts and technologies impact and set the parameters for users' experiences but also (3) how users have agency in navigating and negotiating these times (Keightley & Downey, 2018). For instance, the practice of "checking" (Chapter 2) involves more than a superficial glance at the latest headline: it takes place in a distinct (spatio)temporal context, such as checking one's phone in the morning to postpone having to get up and get ready for work, or filling up the time between two appointments; it is shaped by how the news is presented to the user (e.g. ordered chronologically and/or ranked by importance) and how the device or platform is to be operated; and (as this chapter will show) it is shaped by people's tactics for using the news.

Methodology: a case for experience

As noted, most studies of news use conceptualize time as a given. In this chapter, we focus instead on time as part of people's *experience*: what spending time on news means from a user perspective. Experience is a fruitful point of departure for four reasons. First, it refers to undergoing or having undergone something (Tuan, 1977), and as such helps one move beyond opinions (Costera Meijer, 2013) that are not grounded in people's actual, everyday encounters with news. For instance, for our research purposes it is less helpful to establish whether news users have a particular opinion about time (e.g. that "accuracy" is more important than "immediacy") than to establish and understand how they actually go about checking the latest news.

Second, focusing on the "undergoing" of an experience enables one to capture how the passing of time is integral to people's news use.

Third, experience is a broad concept that opens up the possibility of a wide variety of dimensions related to news use to be included, from cognitive to affective, from communicative to aesthetic, from material to spatiotemporal (Gentikow, 2009, in Ytre-Arne, 2011; see also Costera Meijer, 2016). Following the notion of "zones of intermediacy" (Keightley, 2013), in order to understand what spending time on news means from a user perspective, we must take a broader view that captures how different temporalities overlap and give meaning to an experience. The way news *functions* in people's lives matters here too: does spending 20 minutes on snacking entertainment news versus three minutes on scanning the latest public affairs news mean people find the former more important?

Fourth, taking experience as a point of departure allows for "temporal reflexivity" (Carlson & Lewis, 2018) regarding one's methods and their epistemological consequences. Experience can be described as "a cover-all term for the various modes through which a person knows and constructs a reality" (Tuan, 1977, p. 8). These modes include sensation, perception, and conception (Oakeshott in Tuan, 1977, p. 8).[2] Following Throop's (2003) call for using methods that "differentially access both pre-reflective and reflective varieties of experience. . . [and thus] ensuring that experience is explored ethnographically throughout the entire range of its various articulations" (Throop, 2003, p. 235), we draw from three recent qualitative studies that each center on a different "mode of knowing." The dominant qualitative method, interviewing, typically depends upon what might be called conception: "those explicit reflective processes that tend to give coherence and definite form to experience" (Throop, 2003, p. 235). In order to include a wide array of dimensions related to how people experience spending time on news, we used a different "temporal orientation" in each of our methods. In study #1, participants reflected on an *immediately prior* news experience (conception). In study #2, participants verbally reported their news experience *in real time* while using news (perception). Finally, in study #3, participants were filmed *while* using news and *afterward* watched and reflected on these videos, with the aim of capturing sensory and embodied dimensions of their news use (sensation). Table 4.1 provides further

Table 4.1 Methodological approaches to studying user perspectives on time spent

Study	Method and procedure	Temporal orientation	Dominant mode of knowing
#1 What viewers of current affairs experience as captivating political information (Groot Kormelink & Costera Meijer, 2017)	Viewing and discussing clips: we watched items from current affairs TV shows and immediately afterward interviewed each participant about the extent to which they felt captivated by each item. ($N = 54$)	Reflective	Conception
#2 What clicks actually mean (Chapter 3)	Think-aloud protocol: participants browsed digital news as they normally would and said out loud all the steps they made and thoughts they had. ($N = 56$)	Real-time	Perception
#3 Video-ethnography of people's everyday news use in the home (Chapter 5)	Video-ethnography: participants were filmed from two sides while using news in their own home, on their own devices; immediately afterward the videos were watched and made sense of with each participant. ($N = 13$)	Real-time; reflective	Sensation

details of each study. The aim, thus, was to use different temporal orientations in order to shine light on different dimensions of what it means to spend time using news.

Results

By exploring what spending time means from a user perspective, we generated three main findings that add to our understanding of time (spent) as a measure of news consumption, in particular as it relates to people's interest in, importance attached to, or engagement with news. First, time spent does not reflect the quality of attention. Second, time spent is not necessarily linearly related to interest, attention, or engagement. Third, all time spent is not equal, as different news media and platforms coincide with different temporal experiences.

Finding #1: "time spent" does not reflect quality of attention

Our first finding is that time spent does not reflect *how* that time is spent: the quality of attention. In particular, time spent (measured in minutes or seconds on a page) does not (always) take into account whether users are actively engaging with content (Cherubini & Nielsen, 2016). While perhaps not surprising, our data provide more insight into why this is the case.

First, participants regularly opened news items in new tabs without reading them (yet). When visiting news websites on his laptop, Kevin used the following tactic: first, he scanned the headlines on the homepage and pre-selected potentially interesting articles by using Ctrl + left mouse click to open each article in a new tab. Then, when finished with this pre-selection, he went through the opened tabs one by one, closing each after having read them. This means that each article was open for a considerable time without having been paid any attention to; indeed, the articles that caught his eye first were open the shortest amount of time. In a more extreme example, Myra had a large number of tabs open, some for days, and some which were unlikely to end up being read at all. Myra explained:

> Yes, also very often it's things I don't read. Then I think, "oh I'll read that later" . . . and then there's like 15 things open and then sometimes I don't read them at all, and they're open for like two weeks.

In the latter case, then, articles collecting more "time spent" actually points to Myra's *not* being very interested in reading them.

This complication can partially be overcome by looking at *engaged time*: a more sophisticated metric that measures the time users *actively* spend engaging with an item, for instance by registering scrolling activity (Cherubini &

Nielsen, 2016). However, even this metric is not faultless. Filming Melanie, we observed that as she was visiting a news site, she was simultaneously watching a series on her television. Her gaze constantly shifted between the article she was reading and the TV series. Yet, because she was nonetheless repeatedly "moving" through the article by constantly having her finger on her mouse, even the "engaged time" metric would not have picked up her shifting attention. Here too, her longer "engaged time" was actually the result of her *limited* engagement with and attention to the news.

Time spent thus does not capture the quality of users' attention to news. We also found this in study #1, where we interviewed viewers about their experiences watching items from two different current affairs TV shows. We found a marked difference in how the two shows were watched. One show was appointment television: participants watched it intently in a concentrated, lean-forward fashion, because they wanted to learn about politics. The other show was watched in a lean-back fashion: participants often had it play in the background while doing other activities, paying attention with one ear. Carmen illustrates: "It's on in the background, but then I'm also cooking and [unpacking] the groceries, so doing all kinds of things at home, and then if it's really interesting I will watch a bit." The amount of time spent viewing these shows does not capture the varying levels of attention and interest involved.

It is also worth noting that spending time on news is not a stamp of approval from users, nor does it indicate people attach importance to it. Previous research showed that people consume news that they do not see as quality news (Costera Meijer, 2007), news that does not lead to a satisfying viewing experience (Stanca, Gui, & Gallucci, 2013), and news that they do not trust (Tsfati & Cappella, 2003). Similarly, our participants had no problem admitting that their attention to news did not correspond with their judgment of quality. For instance, Walter (27) criticized the journalistic quality of one news item but watched attentively because it was entertaining: "I think at least television-wise it's well done, and as a result I paid attention." In study #2, which explored why users (do not) click on news (Chapter 3), we similarly found that spending time with funny or sensational news meant participants *enjoyed* rather than *appreciated* it (cf. Bartsch & Schneider, 2014; Oliver & Bartsch, 2010). This was especially the case with "clickbaity" headlines:

> Joe (26): Then I click it if it's a very sensational headline, so I'm more like "oh what the hell" . . . sometimes there are headlines that make you go like "what is this ridiculousness" or "what the hell is that supposed to mean," and then I'm sometimes inclined to click.

Jack (56): "Metal band wants money for music use during torture Guantanamo," then I'm like, god what an item [clicks] then I click it and I think, what kind of band is that, what's the story behind it.

Danny (25): Pretty often NU.nl has these stupid news items about, I don't know, a New Year's Day dive. Couldn't care less, but if it happens to have a picture of a lady, I do click on it.

From a user's perspective, spending time with news is no quality endorsement. As these quotes illustrate, time spent on funny or remarkable news means people find it entertaining, not important or "good."

Finding #2: less time spent can point to not less but more interest or engagement

Earlier we showed that time spent is not an unflawed measure of interest or engagement because it does not capture *how* that time is spent. A perhaps more surprising insight is that shorter news sessions can indicate not the *lack* but the *presence* of interest or engagement. In the methodology section, we listed four reasons for taking experience as the point of departure, one of which was that experience suggests actually *undergoing* something. Study #3 revealed the relevance of an additional meaning of experience: "the ability to learn from what one has undergone" (Tuan, 1977, p. 9). We found three ways in which what we might call people's "being experienced" with news was the reason their news use was so quick or short.

First, "experienced" news users have *embodied knowledge* of how to most efficiently use their devices (see also Chapter 5). Their tactics included quickly swiping downward to refresh and update a news app to see the very latest headlines, rearranging the icons on their smartphone so that their favorite apps are within thumb's reach, and scrolling with a specific finger so they can scroll faster. Consider the extreme detail (and proficiency) in Regina's explanation of why she uses different fingers for different actions on Twitter:

For scrolling et cetera I just use my thumb on Twitter. . . . Sometimes when I'm ALL the way down and I have to go all the way up uhm then it's faster to scroll with my forefinger because . . . with my right hand I hold [my phone] so . . . with my forefinger I have access to the entire screen so that . . . I can make the movement of scrolling to the top bigger, because my reach is larger than with my thumb, because my thumb is not large enough to get all the way to the top of the screen.

More directly related to *time spent*, Ferdinand within seconds decided whether or not a long read he encountered on Facebook was interesting enough to be saved for later. He clicked, scrolled through the article very quickly to pick up words indicating the essence of the article ("When I saw this [section] 'what to do' [it] told me . . . that there was more depth to the news"), clicked on "copy link," opened his Pocket app, and tapped "add" on the latter's pop-up suggestion "Add copied URL to your list?" Although – so he claims – he would read the full article in Pocket later, the "engaged time" metric would register a mere ten seconds spent in the original article. For these experienced users, then, the very quickness of their news use attests to their skills and resourcefulness rather than their disengagement: their sessions were short because they are efficient and proficient in navigating and handling their apps and devices.

Second, more experienced and especially avid news users had "quick" news sessions not because they were uninterested or disengaged but because they were very *efficient* at scanning the environment and picking out new, relevant information. For instance, Robert quickly went through several news app successively. Within each app, he scanned all the headlines added since his last "checking cycle" (Chapter 2) earlier that day and picked out several articles he wanted to read. Within these articles, he was also focused on scanning for new information. He explained:

> If I read things in an item I already know, I tend to skip past it, so I don't read everything in the item because often it contains things that are a repetition of something I had already read elsewhere or [that I] already know.

Such scanning might best be typified as a *burst* of news use: a short, intense session characterized by highly efficient information scanning (cf. Ytre-Arne & Moe, 2018). Here, too, the short time spent points to intense engagement with news rather than superficial engagement or disengagement.

Finally, some participants relied on what we might call their meta-knowledge of news: they are aware of general conventions or title-specific tendencies of the news and adjust their news use accordingly. For instance, Regina referenced the inverted pyramid ("that pyramid model: first the very most important news and then it becomes this little funnel") when explaining why she repeatedly skipped the last paragraphs of news items. Consider also Fiona, who in her e-paper often first reads the lead and the conclusion, and only *then* decides whether it is worth reading the rest of the article. This way she does not waste her time reading what she described as "exaggerated" articles. As she explains:

> I often do that, the beginning and the end, sometimes . . . you read the headline and the conclusion [and that] is enough. Then it's an

enormously suggestive article and then in the end it concludes: it's all not so bad.

She illustrated this when encountering an article about a high-ranking leader of the Taliban being killed. Reading the piece in its entirety would have been a waste of time:

> That bearded dude on the right has been killed, but then I read the beginning [points to the first paragraphs] and then in the end it concludes: his successor is already standing by, then I'm like well [laughs] that's how it goes [laughs]. Then I'm like yeah, this one has been wiped out and the next one is ready, problem is not solved.

Again, here Fiona's and Regina's limited reading time per article points not to their lack of interest or disengagement but to their savviness and experience as news users.

Finding #3: all time spent is not equal

Whereas the first two findings concerned the question of what the metric "time spent" does and does not measure, the third finding relates to the comparability of news use based on time. To be sure, since attention is a finite resource that people can only spend once, time is a most useful measure for studying how people allocate their overall attention between different activities, devices, or platforms. However, what it *means* to spend more time on one medium versus another is a more complicated matter. Indeed, further complicating the duration fallacy (i.e. the assumption that more time means more interesting or more important), our results suggest that the medium or platform used impacts people's temporal experience of news use.

First, while a very rudimentary division, digital news use seems to call up different expectations of time than traditional news use (print newspapers, TV), not necessarily in terms of the immediacy of content but regarding the speed or, to be more precise, the efficiency of the user practice itself. Participants expected quick, smooth user experiences and were frustrated when these were interrupted. This is illustrated by Kevin, who reflecting on a *past* experience recounted a deeply felt frustration concerning an error on the Dutch news site www.NOS.nl:

> Can I leave a complaint with you about the NOS website? Those videos don't load properly anymore, you have to, VERY annoyingly, you have to reload them and then it gives you an error message, reload and only then it works. . . . That's really fucking annoying. . . . No, but it's really been annoying me. Because often it's clips of like 30 seconds and then

I'm like "oh nooo" [throws up hands and rocks back and forth, conveying a physical expression of frustration] . . . then on one page they have three clips and then you keep having to reload and click again and reload and wehhh. . . . I've noticed I'm watching less because of that, then with the third clip I'm like never mind . . . so it does have a negative impact on my news consumption.

While in objective time reloading a page may only takes a few seconds, it apparently felt like a major interruption of his browsing experience. Mangen (2008, p. 412) describes the impatience users experience when using digital media as "an experiential situation bereft of both physical and phenomenological presence." When a digital medium freezes or falters, the technology is brought to the fore and is experienced as an obstruction or intrusion (Mangen, 2008; see also Ihde, 1990). Although a print newspaper, too, can break down and reveal itself as a technology (e.g. when a drop of coffee falls from one's mug onto the paper, making the text suddenly unreadable), digital media experiences are more easily interrupted. Participants' expectations of smoothness were also apparent in study #2, where some did not want to click on videos because they did not want to sit through a commercial, which was seen as an interruption of the flow of their news use. Compared to traditional news use (especially the print newspaper), during digital news use the experience of time seems to become intensified.

Second, different devices and platforms co-produce different temporal experiences. A prime example here is a distinct user practice on Facebook we called "scrolling," characterized by an urge to keep the movement of scrolling going, regardless of one's interest in the content (see Chapter 5). This is illustrated by Ferdinand, who watched a news video on Facebook for only 20 seconds before feeling the urge to move on: "I thought [the video] was really nice but I don't wanna spend too much time doing it." Although he found it difficult to verbalize what exactly made him want to limit his time with content and keep scrolling other than feeling an urge "to keep it going," it appears that the platform – including the way it is navigated and physically handled with one move (a mouse scroll or a thumb scroll) – invites a sense of restlessness that encourages light, quick engagement with content.

A specific affordance of the video-ethnography (study #3) was that it captured, without interruption, the impact of the *passing of time* on news use. The videos showed that as time went by, some participants grew satiated with news, in the sense that they felt they could not absorb any more information. This was especially the case with participants using media that did not let them (as readily) decide *themselves* in which order to consume news items. On news websites and apps, participants selected and read the items they deemed most interesting first and stopped when they had read everything they wanted to read. On the contrary, on devices and platforms where users tended to follow the order suggested by the creator (e.g. newspaper or e-paper) or could not at all choose the order of news items (e.g. Facebook), satiation impacted their selection behavior and reading style (e.g. reading versus scanning) more pronouncedly. For instance, after having read her newspaper (chronologically) for a while, Norah leafed through her newspaper faster and faster and only glanced at headlines. She even skipped articles that she found very interesting, such as an article regarding dark matter:

> I watched the [documentary] series *Cosmos [A Spacetime Odyssey]*, I *find that SUPER interesting* how all of that works, astronomy and physics. *I'd actually want to read that*, but now I'm thinking "*pff, it doesn't fit [into my head] anymore.*" . . . Because then I have to think about dark matter which is already a VERY complicated concept which no one can actually explain what it is, and then I have to read about that now. . . *pff, I can't anymore* [sighs].

She did not read an article she found "super interesting" because gradually she had become satiated: she felt she could not absorb any more information. Similarly, while viewing the recording of his own Facebook scrolling session, Ferdinand noted:

> "Yeah 'cause then I got tired of checking. Yeah this, ah yeah, the *Time* article was about uh uh . . ."
> Interviewer: [tries to read the headline as captured on video] "6 things."
> "Yeah how to get things done. And I thought it could be nice to click on it just yeah for inspiration, but then I was already tired of clicking so [I] just kept scrolling."

Like Norah, Ferdinand came across an article that interested him, but due to having become "tired" of clicking, he did not select it. This suggests that when studying people's selection or time-spending behavior, the "reading order" suggested or enabled by the platform and device must be taken into account, in particular when inferring people's interests or preferences. For news media with a more or less "predetermined" reading order, the passing of time has greater impact: during the beginning of a user's news session, their selection or time-spending behavior might be more indicative of their (lack of) interest than toward the end of that session. That is, news people come across later – regardless of how interesting they find it – is more prone to being skipped due to them having become satiated.

Even when comparing use of the same news medium, time spent is not always revealing. An illustration is the difference between *allocating* one's time *for* news and *restricting* one's time *with* news. Fiona earmarks her Saturday morning for her newspaper. She sees this as a treat, a moment to relax on her day off. Norah, on the other hand, limits her time with her Saturday paper, actively taking time into consideration when reading individual articles:

> And maybe half way [through the article] I'll think, yeah now I get it, let me go on, because I still have a whole newspaper and I don't plan on spending two hours on the newspaper, because I have things to do.

Norah's not wanting to spend too much time on the newspaper is an example of her navigating and negotiating different temporalities, including news delivery time (Saturday morning), leisure time (since it is the weekend, she does not want to spend too much time on "troublesome" things like news), and chore time (having "things to do" like buy groceries). The actual time she spends is insufficient to make sense of this practice: in this "zone of intermediacy" (Keightley, 2013), it is the juncture of these different temporalities that gives her experience its particular meaning.

Conclusion

Aiming to explore what spending time means from a user perspective, this chapter added three nuances regarding "time spent" as a measure of news consumption. Overall, our results confirm a duration fallacy: time spent does not necessarily measure interest in, importance attached to, or engagement with news. First, time spent does not reflect the quality of attention being paid. Second, there is no linear relationship between time spent and interest, importance, or engagement. More time spent on news use can be the result of little interest or engagement, and less time spent can be an indicator of more interest or engagement. The more "experienced" news users tended to engage in quicker news practices exactly because they were "practiced" and skillful at using news: they knew how to handle and navigate their devices, they could efficiently scan digital environments for new and relevant information, and they were aware of news conventions or title-specific tendencies telling them which parts of news articles they could skip. Therefore, discounting news use of fewer than five minutes does not do justice to the intensity and efficiency of the "bursts of news use" we found; these point not to disengaged citizens but to experienced, skillful, inquisitive news users. Third, the experience of time is device and platform dependent. Television and radio are often used in a lean-back mode (Lull,

1990; Larsen, 2000), and reading the newspaper is often experienced as a moment of relaxation, a ritual treat (e.g. Berelson, 1949). With digital news media, on the other hand, speed appears to be valued more, and having to spend more time hinders an efficient experience.

Although time spent is certainly useful to measure how people divide the finite resource that is their attention, our results suggest that we must be mindful of what we can infer from differences between platforms in terms of time spent. This raises questions about what it means that the time people spend on news declines as they move from print to digital (Thurman, 2018; Thurman & Fletcher, 2019). While we share Thurman and Fletcher's (2018, p. 1014) concerns about whether journalism can fulfill its democratic functions "if reading continues to be replaced by glancing and other low-intensity news consumption practices," at the same time our findings problematize the assumption that more time spent on news is inherently desirable. We argue more research is needed to uncover how people's *overall* repertoire of user practices (from scrolling to checking to scanning to reading) jointly inform them of matters of shared concern. As digital news practices as scrolling and checking (can) involve a sense of restlessness and compulsiveness, we also propose further research into the affective qualities of these newer practices (cf. Ytre-Arne & Moe, 2018).

Our results suggest that differences between devices and platforms should also be taken into account when measuring time spent on *individual* (digital) articles. Whereas on news apps users typically select and read articles in succession, on news websites users can open several articles simultaneously. This, first of all, makes it especially urgent to use "engaged time" rather than "time spent" on news websites. What is more, on platforms where users have less (e-paper, paper) or no (perceived) freedom (Facebook, Twitter) to choose their own order of reading, it is important to take into account that readers can grow tired or satiated as their news session progresses. What this implies is that for these platforms, "time spent" becomes a less reliable measure of interest the "further" users are; toward the end of their session they will be more inclined to skip content they do find interesting.

Our results also suggest that a newsroom strategy of retaining users' attention as long as possible may make sense from an attention economy perspective, but does not necessarily match with the experience of (digital) news use which is often (although certainly not always) characterized by smoothness and efficiency. One alternative strategy is to provide news in such a way that it simultaneously affords different user practices, such as "scanning" and "reading" (Chapter 2). For instance, by summarizing a news article in a couple of succinct bullet points, "scanners" are enabled to quickly get the gist of the story while not stopping the "readers" from consuming the full story (indeed, it could be argued that such a schema can also help readers to better understand the core of the article). This strategy maximizes not the time that people spend on the story but the number of people that can get value out of it. Put differently, being attentive to users means enabling a maximum of user efficiency rather than aiming at maximizing time spent. We will further reflect on this in Chapter 6.

A different challenge is how to get news users to take their time to consume content they are already interested in. What the logic of "scrolling" (i.e. "keeping it moving" even if one likes the content) suggests is that users find it (increasingly?) challenging to "commit" to one news item when there is a plethora of other content to consume. One strategy could be to provide content that is experienced as valuable (Costera Meijer, 2020b). The small sample from our video-ethnography tentatively indicates that news users are more willing to invest their time in news that generates insights. For instance, articles that made participants curious about specific but insignificant details were clicked and scanned until the answer was found ("I'm just gonna check which supermarket it was [that was robbed]"), whereas articles that were experienced as more constructive or insightful ("it gave me new insights [and] a broader and richer picture of the issue") tended to be read more fully. This finding is corroborated by our current affairs TV study (study #1), which showed that users were willing to invest their time and attention in exchange for insight into complex political matters. Finally, following the example of the Pocket app, another strategy is to make it easier to save and access articles for later consumption, so that interesting content the user comes across but cannot consume at that moment can be efficiently accessed during a more opportune moment.

It should be emphasized that our findings are based on qualitative research and that quantitative research is needed to establish the frequency of the patterns. For example, we cannot say anything about the prevalence of such practices as efficient information scanning or having multiple tabs with news open at once. Indeed, our aim was to add to our understanding of "time spent" by exploring spending time on news from a user perspective.

Notes

1 This chapter is an updated and revised version of Groot Kormelink, T., and Costera Meijer, I. (2019). A user perspective on time spent: Temporal experiences of everyday news use. Originally published in *Journalism Studies*, *21*(2): 271–286.

2 Whether these modes of knowing are empirically separable is beyond the scope of this chapter; we use them for their heuristic value.

5 Material and sensory dimensions of everyday news use[1]

> It is a weird way of reading, and I THINK that digital medium invites that. . . . You don't have that whole page in front of you so with that mouse you constantly have to select a piece of text.

Our participant Fiona was surprised to learn that when she reads her e-paper on her (large) laptop, she sometimes starts reading in the middle of an article. She reads her e-paper in this unusual way not because she chooses to, but because she uses her mouse to navigate: the text of the e-paper is too small to read without zooming in, but the mouse makes it difficult to "blow up" a specific piece of text. Consequently, she sometimes reads articles in a random, fragmented order. This example illustrates the relevance of taking material and sensory dimensions into account when studying everyday news use. So far, the empirical chapters in this book have focused mostly on what people *do* with news: what practices they engage in and what this means to them. In this chapter, we expand our focus to what news use *feels* like: affectively but also sensorially and especially tactilely. The chapter epigraph illustrates the relevance of broadening our gaze to material and sensory dimensions of news use. To begin with, fragmented reading could have major consequences for people's understanding and interpretation of news.

Yet, within media and journalism studies, the relation between news media as material objects and news users' sensory experiences of them has been virtually overlooked, especially in an everyday context (for exceptions, see Fortunati et al., 2015; Boczkowski et al., 2020). Audience research has focused mostly on the cognition and interpretation of content. Implicitly, news users tend to be conceived of as disembodied, cognitive beings whose devices and platforms are neutral conduits of information. Uses and gratifications theory, for instance, aims to explain how people actively seek out media to fulfill particular social and psychological needs (Katz, Gurevitch, & Haas, 1973), while Hall's (1973) influential encoding/decoding model looks at how people interpret messages. Although studies approaching news use as a ritual focus on the routinized and therefore often automatic character of everyday news practices (Bird, 2011; Couldry, 2004; Madianou, 2009; Silverstone, 1994), here, too, the sensory experiences involved are largely overlooked. In this chapter, we therefore seek to capture the material and sensory dimensions of people's everyday news use and make sense of their significance.

In focusing on materiality and sensory experiences, we answer recent calls for non-representational and non-media-centric approaches to media use (Couldry, 2012; Moores, 2012). Non-representational theory (NRT), as we discussed in Chapter 1, is an umbrella term whose principles include shifting attention from cognition to the pre-cognitive (or non-cognitive), focusing on practices, giving equal weight to (material) things, and stressing affect and sensation (Thrift, 2008). This chapter therefore starts from people's embodied ways of knowing: knowledge they may not be able to produce off the top of their head but "know" in their body (Merleau-Ponty, 1962; Moores, 2015; Pink & Leder Mackley, 2013). As such, the chapter also responds to recent calls for more attention to haptic dimensions of media use (Parisi, Paterson, & Archer, 2017) and the embodied ways of knowing involved (Richardson & Hjorth, 2017). We also draw from post-phenomenology, which is similarly concerned with the relation between technological objects and users' experience of them (Ihde, 2008; Verbeek, 2005). We first describe how we developed a method – the *two-sided video-ethnography* – that makes visible and thus researchable people's tacit, embodied knowledge of their news use. Second, we show how the materiality of devices and platforms and people's sensory, embodied experiences of them influence how they engage with news, in ways even they themselves had not realized. After illustrating additional unexpected findings, we discuss the theoretical, epistemological, and methodological implications of our research.

Studying news use: non-representational, non-media-centric, and non-news-centric

What does taking a non-representational approach to studying news use mean concretely? First, it requires a shift from cognition toward embodied ways of knowing (Moores, 2012; Thrift, 2008). The approach starts from the idea that people "*know as they go*," as their bodies move (and feel) through environments (Ingold, 2011, p. 154). Pink and Leder Mackley (2013) capture the responsive, know-as-they-go character of embodied knowing well when they argue that people's routes and routines are "habitual and learned, known in the body, while part of a process of ongoing, continual learning that . . . is sensitive to the contingencies of the environment and its affordances" (p. 683). These ideas can also be applied to how people (learn how to) use media. Drawing on Merleau-Ponty's (1962, p. 144) "knowledge in the hands," Moores (2014) argues that when people (start to) use a digital medium, they (literally) *feel* their way through the material object itself *and* the online environments to which it provides access. To illustrate, he describes how he has come to know his way around his e-mail inbox just as his hands have gotten to know their way around his keyboard (Moores, 2014). Because such knowledge is embodied and accessed only when put into practice, it is difficult to transfer without being in situ and in process; as a result, this source of knowledge about news use has remained largely untapped.

Second, a non-representational approach shifts attention from how news users make sense of media messages toward people's actual everyday news practices. The shift also aligns with a non-media-centric approach looking at how practices of media use are intertwined with other everyday practices (Couldry, 2012; Moores, 2012). In order to properly grasp how information is received, one must first understand what people actually *do* with, in, and around media (Couldry, 2004). Couldry (2011) proposes three dimensions of audience practice worth looking at: *texture*, "the rhythms, density, and patterning" (p. 223) of people's practices; *contents*, particularly people's trajectories across different media; and *wider uses and purposes* associated with media practices. In line with this, as we argued in Chapter 1, it is also necessary to take a *non-news-centric* approach, as news has grown increasingly interwoven with other types of information, rendering it less useful to study news use as an isolated practice.

The final implications of a non-representational approach to news use concern a focus on both material "things" and people's sensory and affective experiences of them. As noted, the sensory, embodied experience of news use has been especially overlooked. A notable exception is Fortunati et al. (2015), who show how the material qualities of news media impact users' experience. For instance, whereas print represented "pleasantness" to their participants, online media were associated with "a sensation of coldness" (Fortunati et al., 2015, p. 841). They also experienced printed journalism as a finished product versus online news as an ongoing service (Fortunati et al., 2015), which also has implications for the appreciation of content: print news is perceived as "final" and therefore trustworthy, whereas online news is continuously updated and therefore tentative and thus less trustworthy (Costera Meijer & Groot Kormelink, 2016; Doeve & Costera Meijer, 2013). Due to their different physical nature, print newspapers were also manipulated, controlled, and mastered differently than online newspapers (Fortunati et al., 2015). Zerba's (2011) participants noted material disadvantages of print newspapers, including the effort of reading ("flipping pages, holding, folding, and carrying" [p. 602]) and recycling. Benefits of online news seemed to have more to do with the technological affordances of digital media, allowing for instantaneity, up-to-dateness, and interaction (Fortunati et al., 2015; Zerba, 2011). Ytre-Arne (2011) discovered through focus groups that readers of women's magazines associated the glossy print version with feelings of relaxation and comfort, whereas computers were associated with work and clicking was found "annoying and tiresome" (p. 471). Yet, Boczkowski et al. (2020) found that people who do not read print newspapers also derive "particular pleasure in the glossy and shiny tactile experience of digital news" (p. 576), reflecting the advancements made in recent years by news organizations in terms of usability and visual appeal of their digital productions.

Especially relevant to our research is post-phenomenology's notion of "multistability," which recognizes that technologies mediate our experiences and practices by enabling some actions and constraining others, while simultaneously emphasizing that different people can use, manipulate, and interpret technologies in different ways (Ihde, 2008; Rosenberger & Verbeek, 2015). In an effort to move beyond the enable-constrain binary suggested in affordance theory, Davis and Chouinard (2016, p. 241) propose that artifacts can "request, demand, allow, encourage, discourage, and refuse" actions. They also emphasize how people's experiences of affordances depend on their "perception" (awareness) and "dexterity" (knowledge) and on "cultural and institutional legitimacy." Their conceptual vocabulary serves as a helpful starting point for making sense of how news users experience and interact with their news media as material objects.

Developing the two-sided video-ethnography

As Deuze (2011, p. 138) argues, people live "in, rather than with, media", and therefore do not always recognize their own media habits. This makes methods that rely on people's own perceptions and reflections (surveys, interviews, diaries) less suitable for studying material and sensory dimensions of news use – at least the tacit, automatic, and habitual micro-processes we are interested in. Experiments, even those approximating a natural setting (e.g. Kruikemeier et al., 2018; Neijens & Voorveld, 2016; Segijn et al., 2016), are also unsuitable for our research aims because the devices used are not the participants' own, and consequently the *learned* character of embodied knowledge is not captured. The think-aloud protocol partly overcomes these limitations but ultimately is unsuitable because it interrupts the flow of people's news use (cf. Chapter 3). We also tested "video re-enactment," having participants perform their news practices on camera as they normally would while commenting and answering questions from the researcher (Pink & Leder Mackley, 2013). However, this proved less appropriate for our research aims because (1) it interrupted the flow of news use, forcing participants to stop and reflect on movements they usually do very quickly or automatically; and (2) while commenting on their practices, participants used gestures related to the realm of explanation rather than to their news use.

In order to bring material and sensory dimensions of everyday news use into view, a new method was needed. We devised, tested, and refined a method that first captures people's news use in real time and then allows them to "look in" and reflect on it (cf. Lahlou, 2011): the "two-sided video-ethnography." It consists of five steps. First, we filmed participants from *two* sides simultaneously while they used news: a frontal perspective to capture participants' position, posture, gestures, and expressions, and an over-the-shoulder perspective to capture the content of the news as well as people's trajectories in and physical handling of their devices. Second, we watched and made sense of the videos with each participant individually, having them comment on and clarify their actions. Third, we analyzed the videos and transcripts. The analysis was characterized by constant comparison between data and analysis (cf. Corbin & Strauss, 1990). Following post-phenomenology, our research process started from first-person experience (as is central to phenomenology), but also included "intersubjective checking and critique," making it "experiential, but not 'subjectivistic'" (Ihde, 2008, p. 6). This collaborative nature of our analysis proved important: discussing interpretations of the data between researchers significantly moved forward the analysis. Fourth, we shared our interpretations with the participants to see if they could elaborate on them. This step proved especially helpful for making sense of the significance of our participants' practices and (micro-) gestures. Finally, we adapted and improved our analyses accordingly.

We combined the two-sided video-ethnographies with day-in-your-life interviews, which were held immediately prior to filming. Participants were asked to take the researcher through a typical day of news use: "Imagine it's morning, your alarm goes off. What is the first moment you encounter news?," followed repeatedly by "What is the next moment you encounter news?" Going through their day chronologically allowed participants to envisage their news use, resulting in a vivid account of their news routines. Whereas video-ethnography was useful for zooming in on "hidden" dimensions, the day-in-the-life method captured overall patterns of news use.

We selected 13 participants through purposeful sampling (Patton, 1990). As we are especially interested in material and sensory dimensions of news use, we selected participants to include a variety of devices (newspaper, computer, smartphone, tablet, TV) and platforms (website, app, e-paper, Facebook, Twitter) (see Table 5.1). We opted for a location where we could

Table 5.1 Participants in two-sided video-ethnography

Participants			Filmed news practice(s)		
Name (anonymized)	Age	Gender	Device	Platform/title	Length (filmed news practice only)
Kevin	29	M	Smartphone	News app (NOS)	00:12:56*
			Print newspaper	*De Volkskrant*	00:27:02
Norah	31	F	Print newspaper	*Het Parool*	00:50:03*
			Tablet	E-paper (*Het Parool*)	00:22:29
Ferdinand	30	M	Smartphone	Facebook (app)	00:11:02
Regina	29	F	Smartphone	News app (Nu.nl); Twitter (app)	00:08:11
Julie	28	F	Laptop	Websites (Facebook, news sites, other)	00:09:14
Martin	32	M	Smartphone	News app (Nu.nl); Instagram (app)	00:03:27
Fiona	60	F	Laptop	E-paper (*De Volkskrant*)	00:21:45
			Print newspaper	*NRC Handelsblad*	00:16:50
Joanne	32	F	Print newspaper	*De Gelderlander*	00:17:16
Robert	31	M	Smartphone	News apps (multiple)	00:13:52
Melanie	28	F	Laptop	Websites (blogs, *De Correspondent*)	00:24:16
Myra	29	Non-binary	Computer	Websites (Facebook, blogs, other)	00:27:42
Marie	29	F	Television	NOS Journaal (Morning bulletin)	00:08:56
Layla	31	F	Television	NOS Journaal (Morning bulletin)	00:08:56

* Indicates "video re-enactment" (test phase) and therefore includes time spent on (contemporaneous) commentary by participant and researcher.

easily capture diverse news practices: the home. Our approach was user-centered: we filmed only those practices participants actually engage in, including *when* and *where* they engage in them. Participants were selected from and through our social circle. First, a "relationship of trust" (Madianou, 2010, p. 434) is necessary when engaging in ethnography, especially when filming people during intimate moments, including in the morning while wearing pajamas. Second, because the research process (including the day-in-your-life interview, filming the practice(s), watching and discussing the recordings) is time-consuming, participants must be willing to put in time and effort. Third, because we shared our findings with our participants, sometimes repeatedly, it was important that they were easily reachable. All participants live in the Netherlands, a country characterized by high internet penetration (95%) and online news use (79%) at the time (Newman et al., 2018). The limitations of this selection process are abundantly clear. Most notably, our sample is dominated by young, well-educated people. However, our goal is not to be representative but to explore the various material and sensory dimensions involved in everyday news use.

Results

First, our method enabled us to capture the sensory, embodied experiences of our participants. As evidenced by their use of such phrases as "I hadn't realized," the video-ethnography made visible and thus discussable tacit, habitual, and automatic dimensions of their news use. Especially notable were the subtle micro-gestures involved in efficiently handling and navigating their devices. Their hands were often future-oriented, already anticipating the next move, even while their cognitive focus was still directed toward the information at hand. A common example is how the participants already grabbed the lower-right corner of the newspaper while still reading the current page. When asked about this, Joanne suspected she did this because "while reading you can easily already do that, you don't have to think about it and then when you're ready you can *immediately* move on." Similarly, after Kevin turned his phone horizontally to make the news video he was watching go full screen, he turned it back vertically before the video had finished, explaining that he was "already anticipating that I go back to the list [of headlines]." Robert swiped his left forefinger upward shortly after opening a news app on his smartphone to ensure he saw the very latest headlines.

Material matters

Capturing the material and sensory aspects of news use matters because, first, the way our participants (physically) handle news devices and interfaces affects how they engage with news. Their devices and platforms invite or inhibit participants' actions in ways they themselves were usually not aware of. This was most evident in the example that opened this chapter: Fiona's use of her print newspaper and her e-paper (read on her laptop). Similar to the respondents in Neijens and Voorveld's (2016) experiment, Fiona initially believed her reading style on both versions was the same: reading and skimming through articles linearly. While watching the recording of her e-paper use with her, however, we discovered that her mouse use impacted her reading style: she sometimes zoomed in and started reading at a seemingly random part of an article. When asked to clarify, she explained:

> It is a weird way of reading, and I THINK that digital medium invites that. . . . You don't have that whole page in front of you so with that mouse you constantly have to select a piece of text. . . . Do you get what I mean? Because of that zooming in with that mouse you constantly get a little piece of text, you have the tendency to constantly select a little piece.

Fiona reads e-paper articles in a fragmented way, not because she desires or chooses to, but because the combination of her e-paper, her laptop, and her mouse "demands" it (Davis & Chouinard, 2016). By contrast, in her print newspaper she reads and skims articles linearly.

Second, the sensory and tactile dimensions involved in using *platforms* and their interfaces also affect how our participants physically engage with them and the content they contain. The most prominent example of this is the movements and micro-gestures involved in using Facebook. Indeed, as discussed in Chapter 2, we identified a distinct user practice our participants engaged in Facebook: "scrolling." Scrolling is their default mode for Facebook on both smartphone and laptop, described by our participants in terms of a desire or, more precisely, an *urge* to "keep it going." Ferdinand, when asked why he made certain choices on Facebook, kept using phrases like "so let's just keep it going" and "so I just kept scrolling." Even stopping or pausing was experienced as an interruption:

> Should I click on the page? Because maybe there is something more interesting to read, but then I was just too *impatient* and *I kept scrolling, I didn't want to stop.*

The video-ethnography allowed us to capture the embodied impatience associated with scrolling. Twenty seconds after Ferdinand did click on a video, he briefly touched the screen to see how long the video was. When asked about this, he described this was not because he was bored, but rather because he longed to get back to the feed and keep it going:

> Yeah that moment I was already getting impatient and *wanted to move on*. . . . I thought [the video] was really nice but *I don't wanna spend too much time doing it*. This is the moment I remember thinking that I was like "ok, the information that I wanted is already [passed], *so I can keep scrolling*" but then I was like no maybe there is. . .

Ferdinand also described getting out of the scrolling flow as laborious. Upon encountering a BBC post in his feed, he hesitated for a moment, contemplating whether to visit the BBC page before scrolling on. Asked why he had not clicked, he answered: "Too much work [laughs]."

Similarly, Julie paused at a Facebook video that started playing automatically, but then she moved on because it didn't have any subtitles and she didn't want to click the sound button. This was not because she did not want to make noise, but because clicking was laborious:

> If there'd been text at the bottom . . . I would've been more triggered to stay, you know, then I can consume the news without having to actually do ANOTHER action.

Apparently, when scrolling, one click is already considered too much work. It appears participants do not want to leave the flow of scrolling and feel they must get back to their feed as soon as possible when they do get out of it. Both participants stopped their scrolling practice when they became "bored" (Julie) or "tired" (Ferdinand).

(In)experience and mastery

It is important to emphasize that while devices and platforms invite or demand certain uses, our participants also use and manipulate them in ways beyond their creators' intention. Some participants showed fargoing mastery of their devices and platforms through their manual dexterity. In Chapter 2 we mentioned how Regina was very conscious of the publicness of her social media practices. When we visited her again a few years later for the video-ethnography, we noticed how this carefulness translated into different ways of physical handling her (social media) apps. Regina used different fingers when *clicking* within her news app (right thumb) versus her Twitter app (left forefinger). Emphasizing that she had been unaware of this, she explained that Twitter requires her to "click a little more precisely" to avoid accidently liking or retweeting a post. When *scrolling*, through both Facebook ("I pretty much only scroll on Facebook") and Twitter, she instead used her right thumb; except when she wants to quickly jump to the "top" of Twitter – then she uses her left forefinger because it works faster. Her micro-gestures are so natural and automatic to her that the smartphone has become an extension of her body, enabling her to optimize her news practices also in terms of time investment (see Chapter 4). The Dutch expression for mastering something, *het in de vingers krijgen* ("getting it in the fingers"), certainly applies here.

For other participants, it was their lack of experience and mastery that shaped their news experience. This is illustrated by Norah, who had recently subscribed to a weekend paper. Reading it on Saturday morning, she became "satiated" after reading the first ten pages or so. The recording shows how she started leafing through the paper faster and faster, grabbing the corner of the next page as soon as she had turned the previous one. She explained that at this point she was only scanning headlines. Notably, she *did* come across articles she did want to read, especially in the arts and science sections, but by that time, she had run out of time and concentration. When asked why she did not start with these sections that most appealed to her, she said this had simply never occurred to her: "It's so ingrained in your mind, you start a book at the beginning too and then you leaf through it. You don't start in the middle." It was not the newspaper's particular materiality (print) that demanded this chronological order. When two weeks later we filmed Norah's use of the same title's e-paper version on her tablet, she (apparently having forgotten the researcher's suggestion) similarly remarked: "By the time I'm on page 18 about arts and media . . . I'm actually already like so *pfff* tired of it that I go through it very quickly, so actually they should have this [section] at the beginning."

Following a (predetermined) sequence was due to Norah's dominant reading practice of fiction and her *inexperience* as a newspaper reader. She read the paper as a book ("you start a book at the beginning . . . and then you leaf through it"), and consequently it did not occur to her to follow an idiosyncratic route, the way more experienced newspaper readers might. Kevin, for instance, started with his weekend paper's lighthearted supplement because he wanted to go "from easy to difficult." Norah had neither the "perception" nor the "dexterity" to use these affordances of the newspaper (Davis & Chouinard, 2016). Instead, she seamlessly tapped into her knowledge of fiction reading. This negatively affected her reading experience, as she felt she needed to go through the "bad" news on the first pages in order to get to the lighter supplements.

Norah's inexperience with the e-paper also negatively impacted her experience in a different way. Unaware of the option to make articles instantly more readable by clicking on them, she (again tapping into her knowledge of fiction reading) zoomed in on articles as if moving the page closer to her face. The recording shows her continuously making wrong gestures while trying to zoom in and out. Once she even accidently "zoomed out" of the entire newspaper, which put her back at the front page, much to her frustration (and instead of jumping straight to the page she had zoomed out of, she – rather tellingly – again swiped through the entire paper to get there). In the follow-up interview she admitted she had not given the e-paper enough of a chance "to get used to it." As Tuan (1977, p. 9) notes, becoming experienced "requires that one venture forth into the unfamiliar and experiment with the elusive and the uncertain." For Norah, the e-paper was not worth this effort.

Deepening news user practices

In addition to shedding light on the interaction between news as material object and its users, capturing the material and sensory dimensions of news use also enables a fuller, deeper understanding of previously discovered everyday news user practices as discussed in Chapter 2. Following Moores (2012, 2015), we found the concepts of "wayfaring" and "inhabitant knowledge" (Ingold, 2000) particularly helpful. Consider Julie, who uses her laptop for news online through a practice we previously called "snacking": consuming bits and pieces of information in a relaxed, easygoing fashion to gain a sense of what is going on (Chapter 2). By minutely following her movements, we realized this easygoingness is in fact actively evoked and maintained. She manages her mood (Zillmann, 1988) by following familiar routes (visiting "feel good" websites) and expertly slaloming around negative content. While seemingly effortless, these movements in fact require *experience* and *skill*. First, Julie explores these online environments responsively, skillfully "feeling" her way as she goes, both sensorially and affectively. When she watched a video on Facebook about Rio de Janeiro (which she had visited), she moved on as soon as she realized it was about pickpockets being beaten up: "Everything I experience as negative I scroll through as quickly as possible, because I don't want to, I don't need to experience that." Indeed, she selectively *avoids* certain types of news based on valence (see Chapter 2). It is worth emphasizing that feeling here refers to both Julie's emotional state and the movements of her hand: she quickly scrolled away when the news "hit" her. Second, by routinely visiting a set of "feel good" websites, Julie has come to "inhabit" these online environments in the sense that she has learned exactly where to go to find the typical content she desires when snacking the news.

Wayfaring is like making a forest your own: not only do you learn which routes to use, but you also gain knowledge of its characteristics so you can make better choices as you go. It is not limited to any material: users can also create their own routes through newspapers (e.g. by starting at their favorite section). Yet we did find that participants who used news websites on computers and laptops "roamed" more freely. Myra, for instance, repeatedly and effortlessly switched between websites, using the constantly visible URL bar to jump to different websites and the tabs in the browser as shortcuts to their favorite "spots." Participants who used news apps on their smartphones, on the other hand, visited them in succession, moving onto the next one only when they were done with the previous one. The material characteristics of news media, then, seem to afford different forms of movement. We might say that websites, by the mere availability and visibility of URL bars and tabs, "allow" constant change of direction making them more suitable for snacking, whereas apps "discourage" (Davis & Chouinard, 2016) this as it takes effort to do so (closing one app and opening another).

Smartphone: seducer and enricher

Another news user practice deepened through our video-ethnography was "reading," which is done individually, with great attention, in longer sessions (Chapter 2). An eye-opener in particular was how interruptions from one's smartphone can be experienced as an extension of the news practice rather than a distraction. On Saturday morning, Kevin aims to be fully immersed in the paper: "I try to force myself to not divide my attention between everything, multitasking is an illusion. . . . I'm like, otherwise I shouldn't do it, . . . then there's no point." However, when we watched his recording, we saw that during his 24-minute reading session, he grabbed his phone three times:

1   To take a picture of an exhibition so he would remember it when later scrolling through his photo gallery (after which he checked his WhatsApp messages);
2   To take a picture of a headline and send it to a friend;
3   To check a push notification that made his phone buzz: he received a WhatsApp message and went on to check several group chats.

It might be tempting to conclude (as we initially did) that Kevin's reading practice was repeatedly interrupted by his smartphone. This is certainly true for the third time, when the phone demanded Kevin's attention by buzzing. Here Kevin described his phone as "seducing" him when he is less focused. His phone represents an ongoing stream of social information that apparently is hard to get away from. Stone (n.d.) coined the term "continuous partial attention," which she described as "motivated by a desire to be a LIVE node on the network."

However, in his follow-up interview Kevin clarified that he did *not* experience his first two interactions with his phone as interruptions. On the contrary, he saw them as "an extension" of the practice of reading, comparable to looking up an unclear term when reading news online. Illustrating the importance of asking users themselves how they experience technology and its affordances, Kevin's smartphone both "demanded" interruption and "allowed" (Davis & Chouinard, 2016) extension of his newspaper reading.

While still done individually, with great attention, in longer sessions, Kevin's reading is imbued with multiple social micro-processes that enrich his experience. His practice also emphasizes that as reading is about immersion, it is less about effective information processing than about allowing oneself the time to fully enjoy one's (ritual) practice, far beyond merely engaging with the text itself.

Minutely following Kevin's actions also allowed us to uncover (details of) the practice "sharing" that might be hard to capture with other methods. The recording showed him taking a picture of a news article and sending it to a friend using WhatsApp. As we looked more closely, the researcher noticed that the picture showed only a headline; it did not contain any other text his friend could actually read. Only when asked about this, Kevin said he knew his friend would never read the article, nor did he himself have any interest in reading it, but he just wanted to share that he had come across something his friend had mentioned a while ago. In the follow-up interview, Kevin further clarified that sharing the headline was not about sharing actual content; rather, it was about "just connecting" with his friend. This form of news sharing is an example of "phatic communications," where "the connection to the other . . . becomes significant, and the exchange of words becomes superfluous" (Miller, 2008, p. 395).

Bycatch: making home through news

Through our two-sided video-ethnography we also generated insights that do not directly relate to the material, sensory angle of this chapter but that do concern affective dimensions of news use, therefore fitting within a non-representational approach. Specifically, we found the notion of place-making very helpful for understanding the significance of news use in people's home. Place-making describes how people, through their repeated practices and routines, eventually come to feel familiar in and ascribe meaning to environments (Ingold, 2000; Pink, 2012; Tuan, 1977). What we found is that news use not only co-constitutes place (Peters, 2012) but that people through their news practices also *create* a sense of space – of home. Seamon (1979, p. 70) defines "at-homeness" as "the usually unnoticed, taken-for-granted situation of being comfortable in and familiar with the everyday world in which one lives," but in the context of this chapter we also use the concept more literally to denote feelings of warmth, safety, and comfort people (can) associate with being inside their home. Our participants created a sense of home – or, in the words of Pink and Leder Mackley (2013), made their home "feel right" – through news in various ways, such as taking the time to fully immerse oneself in the beloved ritual of reading the newspaper (Fiona) or watching the morning news in bed to engage in a shared activity (Layla and Marie). These findings align with the ritual and thus (ultimately) reassuring function of news that is often emphasized (Silverstone, 1994). Yet, for some participants news played a more ambiguous role, sometimes also disrupting their feeling of at-homeness. We discuss two examples here.

Norah's video-ethnography uncovered an intriguing paradox between an ideal picture in her head that reading the weekend paper she had recently subscribed to "should" invoke and her actual experience while reading it. When she gets up on Saturday morning, she first makes breakfast, which she eats in bed while watching a series on Netflix. She was adamant about not reading the newspaper in bed; this space is reserved for "nice things instead of the troublesome things that news usually is." Only afterward does she grab the newspaper from the cabinet in the hallway – where her roommate has left it for her – and put it on her living table.

> Because I think a newspaper belongs on the table, I just already think that's nice, like, you have a cozy living room and the fresh newspaper from today that is laying so beautifully crackling, unopened on the table waiting for me . . . and I grab a cup of coffee with it.

Spreading the newspaper out on her living room table is a place-making activity: it helps create a "cozy living room." Her phrasing "*belongs* on the table" implies that this is the correct way to read the newspaper. Despite noting the paper's "troublesome" content, Norah compared (when asked) her Saturday morning newspaper ritual to a breakfast buffet:

> In other words, there is a lot and you pick out the nice things that seem attractive to you and those you sit at the table to nicely read it, to munch on.

Her use of the words "attractive" and "nice" implies that reading the paper is a pleasurable activity. Her actual experience while reading suggests, however, that this ritual is an ideal she aspires to rather than a practice she enjoys herself. Most notably, she tried to skip negative content because it did not fit her sought-after mood on Saturday:

> Because here I'm already reading that 16% of women are raped, here I read that people are dying of hunger, you know, it is Saturday and I kind of have to keep my good spirits a bit. I'm a bit egotistical in that perhaps, but well, you can't carry all the suffering in the world on your shoulders.

Her justification for skipping negative content that "it is Saturday" is significant. We argue that limiting her engagement with negative news can be interpreted as having a "place-making" as well as "*time*-making" function. She aims to construct a Saturday morning experience after a particular ideal picture of it: a time she apparently is supposed to be "in good spirits." News about suffering does not fit this picture. Norah also "makes time" by restricting her time with the paper. Whereas some other participants saw reading the paper as a treat, a moment to relax that they *allocated* time for, Norah *restricted* her time: she wants to spend a maximum of 30–45 minutes, and was acutely aware of the passing of time:

> Now that I'm discussing this consciously, I'm thinking jeez, it's pretty important what's on the first ten pages, because you kind of lose your attention and think, well, it's Saturday, we've already been reading for 45 minutes, I'm in the mood to go out to do things, go to the store.

Again she used Saturday as an explanation. She wanted to finish reading the paper and do what she was in the mood for: to go out.

The disconnect between the way Norah romanticized the ritual of Saturday morning reading and her less-than-enthusiastic actual experience suggests that rather than being inherently interested in reading the news, it was the practice itself and its supposedly place-making qualities that she valued. When carefully probed in our follow-up interview, Norah said that one of the reasons she subscribed to the newspaper was that it would be "homely, because of course back in the day at home with your parents you always had the newspaper too," referring to her parents' cozy practice of reading the weekend paper at the kitchen table. Quite literally, Norah had thought of the newspaper as a homemaker. More than modeling after her parents' news habits (Edgerly et al., 2018), her attempt at this Saturday morning ritual was an effort to (re)create a sense of home on a fundamental level: the nostalgia of yesteryear. However, the actual act of reading the newspaper disrupted this homemaking. Norah eventually cancelled her subscription.

Safe space from which to venture out

News can also help create a sense of home in a different way. Here, we return to an example discussed in Chapter 1. When Melanie arrives back from work, she divides her attention between *The Gilmore Girls* (*GG*) – a show she has seen several times – on her TV (Netflix) and news sites and blogs on her laptop. The recording shows Melanie averting her eyes constantly from laptop to TV and vice versa, revealing that she did not read any article from start to finish. Rather, she alternated reading parts of articles with catching parts of *GG*. Melanie's news practice, thus, is characterized by fragmentation – even though one of the sites she visits is Dutch news website *De Correspondent*, which typically has longer pieces one would assume to require a more concentrated mode of reading. When asked, Melanie explained she finds the news "too serious" to fully engage with, but she does "want to just check everything." Watching *GG* is also a fragmented activity: she only looks up when her favorite characters (Rory's circle) are on her TV screen, and goes back to her laptop screen when less favorite characters (like Emily) appear. Dividing her attention is not about "continuous partial attention" (Stone, n.d.), multitasking, or being efficient. Rather, rewatching *GG* creates a nice, homely, nostalgic, predictable, reassuring atmosphere that could best be described as "ontological security" (Giddens, 1991). In her follow-up interview, Melanie confirmed that rewatching *GG*, unlike trying a new series, provides the homeliness and predictability she desires. The show is like a warm blanket from under which she can *then* safely peek into or have a sense of connection with the "serious" public world.

Conclusions

In this chapter we capture and make sense of the material and sensory dimensions of everyday news use by employing a two-sided video-ethnography. Our first conclusion is that users are not only coaxed into certain behavior by carefully designed interfaces (Van Dijck, 2013), but that news devices and platforms also invite and inhibit different ways of *physically* (and often *manually*) handling and navigating them, resulting in different ways of engaging with news content. It is important to emphasize that our participants were typically unaware of this until we watched and discussed the recordings of their own news use.

Second, news users' mastery of devices and platforms – or lack thereof – influences how optimized their news practices are in terms of time investment. Consequently, time can no longer be assumed to be an unproblematic indicator of people's attention or interest in news: the more "practiced" the user, the more efficient their news use (see Chapter 4).

Our third conclusion is that whether and how people make use of technologies' affordances is not only shaped by their perception and knowledge of the technology in question (Davis & Chouinard, 2016) but also their (prior) experience with *different* technologies. Note the participant who – against her wishes, in retrospect – read through both her print and e-paper chronologically, because she projected her book reading experiences onto them; she had been "primed" to read linearly. This example makes a non-news-centric approach especially relevant, not only for studying the adoption and "incorporation" (i.e. embodiment) of new news devices and platforms but also for seeing whether news content is accorded its weight.

Fourth, contrary to the common assumption that smartphones distract from newspaper reading (as we also presumed), they are also used as to enrich or extend the reading experience. This finding highlights the value of checking one's interpretations with the research participants in question.

Fifth, we discovered the new distinct user practice of *scrolling*, marked by a strong, embodied urge to keep up the movement of the hand and to not interrupt this flow by (what is experienced as) the laborious act of clicking, even when the user finds the content appealing. This low-intensive, lean-backward user practice calls for more attention to what it means when people (say they) use Facebook for news (Newman et al., 2018). Does it just pass by without making an impression, do they glance for a quick impression, or do they really pay attention (Kümpel, 2020; Wieland & Kleinen-von Königslöw, 2020)?

Sixth, we found that people through their news practices actively *make place* and *time*. Especially notable were participants' coping strategies that mediated between the comforting ritual character of news practices and the disruptiveness of (negative) news content, such as expertly slaloming around disturbing news or "dampening the shock" by simultaneously watching reruns of familiar TV shows. Whereas research has looked into motivations for news use (most notably through uses and gratifications research) and news avoidance (e.g. Toff & Nielsen, 2018; Zerba, 2011), the domain in between, where people – apparently rather meticulously – measure and negotiate their exposure to and engagement with news, has received less attention (for exception, see Couldry & Markham, 2008; see also Chapter 2 where we distinguish between avoiding and abstaining).

Epistemologically, people's lack of awareness about their news use raises concerns about knowledge generated through methods that rely on people's own recollection (surveys, interviews, diaries, etc.). Less worried about social desirability – our participants seemed to have little problem watching cat videos or swiping straight to entertainment news – we were surprised by the irregularities between people's perception of their news practices from just minutes earlier and what the recordings showed. While it is well-known that people have a limited ability to accurately estimate their own news behavior, our participants sometimes wrongly recalled even basic elements of their news use, such as how much of and even which articles they had read. This makes grasping the phenomenological experience of using news even *more* important: only then can people's (systematic) blind spots regarding their own news use be taken into account. Finally, in order to understand and measure how users' handling and navigation of devices and platforms impacts their cognition and sense-making of news, rather than approximating a natural setting, more in situ research is needed: people should be studied using the devices and platforms they *actually* use, *when* and *where* they actually use them.

Note

1 This is a revised and updated version of Groot Kormelink, T., and Costera Meijer, I. (2019). Material and sensory dimensions of everyday news use. Originally published in *Media, Culture & Society*, *41*(5), 637–653.

6 How to deal with news user practices, preferences, and pleasures? From audience responsiveness to audience sensitivity

Knowing how to deal with changing news use is crucial for the survival of news organizations. In this concluding chapter, we reflect on the overarching lessons of the previous chapters for journalistic practice. First of all, it is important to make a distinction between advertising-based and audience-based business models of journalism. In an advertising-based model it might make sense to strive for maximizing users' attention by generating as many clicks, attention minutes, comments, and shares as possible. For news media that want to provide the information users truly appreciate, for public service news media, and for subscription-, member-, and donation-based news media, optimizing for users' *appreciation* might be a more appropriate objective. Getting insight into what kind of journalism people find worth their time and money has become even more urgent since the advertising market took a further hit during the COVID-19 pandemic. This adds further priority to procuring income directly from audiences. Although willingness to pay for digital news remains low (Chyi & Ng, 2020; Goyanes, Demeter, & de Grado, 2020; Newman et al., 2019), there is some evidence that news organizations that provide special value to users do comparatively well in reader-based revenue. Local Norwegian newspapers retain some of the highest readership in the world, by playing "a key role in preserving a sense of local community identity" (Hatcher & Haavik, 2014, p. 149). Swedish newspaper *Dagens Nyheter* saw their digital subscribers overtaking their print subscribers in 2019 by focusing on attracting subscribers with quality journalism (Southern, 2019). According to its head of editorial development, Martin Jönsson, "we show where we give value, it's more positive. For us, it's important to attract with quality of content" (Southern, 2019). In the Netherlands, quality newspapers have retained more of their subscribers than popular newspapers over the past years (Bakker, 2018). The *Guardian* also saw a substantial increase in subscriptions and financial contributions from readers, making it financially sustainable for a second year in a row in 2020 (Waterson, 2020). In times of crisis, quality journalism seems to prove its "worthwhileness" (Schrøder, 2015): during the COVID-19 pandemic,

Dutch quality media gained digital subscribers at an unprecedented pace (van Dongen, 2020). Magazine The *Atlantic* (United States) also gained 36,000 digital subscribers in one month, likely due to its excellent pandemic coverage (Scire, 2020).

We have suggested in the previous chapters that although professional and scholarly attention to audiences has grown enormously, a genuine audience turn in journalism and journalism studies is needed to avoid systematic bias and to truly understand what journalism means from a user perspective. The heart of a genuine audience turn is taking a holistic approach to news use: in this book we have tried to do justice to the full story, the "life world" (what Edmund Husserl calls *Lebenswelt*) of our informants. We have examined closely how news use presents itself through experience, encompassing the complexities and intricacies of personal life. Our analysis was focused on conceptually clarifying what humans live through in situations of news use, including "embodied, practical, emotional, spatial, social, linguistic, and temporal aspects" (Wertz et al., 2011, p. 127).

As we argued in Chapter 1, a genuine audience turn in journalism and journalism studies means replacing "how to *reach* people" with "how to be of *service* to them" (see Costera Meijer, 2013, 2021a). This means finding alternative ways to investigate and become sensitive to the practices, preferences, and pleasures of audiences. Becoming more knowledgeable about what they appreciate about journalism, where, and how, serves as a good starting point. It is worth clarifying that our focus on what people appreciate does not mean that we underestimate the time people spend with (in their own view) less important or entertaining news. We acknowledge the relaxation or diversion function of news for people, but we have also found that people seldom visit a news site or news app, watch a news show, or read a newspaper solely for entertainment purposes. Entertainment, our participants argue, we can find elsewhere (and also better), but we use news because it provides the kind of information worth our time and money. When people consume news items to update themselves, to really understand what happens, to amuse themselves, to relax during a break, or to introduce funny or bizarre facts as conversation topics, they are aware of their distinctive meanings. What we can measure are the different topics, headlines, journalistic genres, or formats people appear to show an interest in. What cannot easily be traced or measured digitally is the kind of interest (entertaining, ritualistic, communicative, and/or informative) or the reasons why they show an interest (as a professional, as a sports fan, as someone not wanting to be excluded from conversations among family/colleagues, etc.). For instance, while for one user visiting a beauty blog is about creating a moment of leisure, for another the same website offers essential professional information. Similarly, when John (41) scrolls through a news app or website during his lunch break. Without clicking he scans the important headlines and leads and updates himself about what happens in the world; this does not take him much time or effort because he is an experienced, well-informed news user. The items he does click one are the funny stuff (stupid and foolish, but nice to know and mood lifting) and sports news which is a hobby of his but not important "in the grand scheme of things." As we explained in previous chapters, audience metrics such as clicks and time spent are susceptible to the frequency fallacy and the duration fallacy. Although his clicking and time-spending behavior suggests that he is interested in entertainment and sports news – which is not incorrect – they tell only a part of the story of what he appreciates about journalism. The attention John pays to what he himself acknowledges as "the important stuff" remains mostly untraceable for news organizations. What he appreciates about the news site is the way it accommodates his various user practices: it presents him with the urgent news in such a way that it can be easily checked and scanned when he wants an update and provides him the "nice to know" stuff for relaxation.

In this concluding chapter, we wrap up the knowledge gained in the previous chapters to address the usefulness of the practice and concept of *audience sensitivity* for news media and journalism scholars to keep up with people's changing news and unchanged news experiences.

What is audience sensitivity?

First of all, audience sensitivity differs from audience responsiveness. Audience responsiveness starts from a journalistic or organizational perspective: "there is a professional response to a more demanding public, a more commercial response to a volatile consumer and a response reflecting the more populist discourse" (Brants & de Haan, 2010, p. 415). It emphasizes the *professional* motives to take the public more seriously and can be seen as a *precondition* for becoming more sensitive to the needs and wants of audiences. Brants and de Haan (2010) call attention to three motives: civic responsiveness, or feeling "a sense of co-responsibility for the well-being of the socio-political system and the democratic process"; strategic responsiveness, described as the motive to persuade "the public, binding them as consumers to the product on offer"; and empathic responsiveness, referring to siding "with a public that traditionally has had no voice in the media" (pp. 416–418).

To be worth people's while (cf. Schrøder, 2015), journalists may have to become sensitive to more dimensions than the three professional motives mentioned by Brants and de Haan (2010). Therefore, the conceptual framework of audience sensitivity therefore starts out from the perspective of the audience or news user and what *they* appreciate about journalism. As we noted in Chapter 1, developing audience sensitivity means that journalists become aware of and get sensitive to what makes news worth their while, including the *infrastructure of news use.*

Becoming sensitive to what the audience appreciates may not work as a distinctive motive or goal. We approach audience sensitivity as a professional *value* that cannot be reached but is lived as part of journalism professionals' (and scholars') everyday work. It is a professional *sensitivity* underlying the whole of our actions: audience sensitivity resonates in the ways scholars do research and how journalists select, present, and produce journalism. In previous chapters we suggested how journalism studies as a discipline or academic field can benefit from such a perspective, but in this concluding chapter we focus on the specific challenges of audience sensitivity for news organizations and journalism professionals. We introduce three dimensions of audience sensitivity. First, we address audience sensitivity as a professional *skill* to facilitate the infrastructure of news use. Second, we discuss audience sensitivity as a professional *alertness*: being wary of and attentive to the underlying logics of metrics. Third, we introduce audience sensitivity as professional *knowledge*: taking into account the affective and sensory dimensions of news use.

Audience sensitivity as facilitating the infrastructure of news use

Once journalists and news organizations realize how people's news use turns out to be substantially more varied than is often assumed, they can aim to provide a better service to their audiences. Developing this *skill* means first of all becoming aware of the "infrastructure" of news use: how news functions and impacts as well as differs in terms of intensity, efficiency, intentness, urgency, rhythm, and pleasure.

The 24 user practices that we distinguish call for a different facilitation of infrastructure. Highly intense, lean-forward user practices such as *reading, watching,* and *listening* are about taking (or making) the time to engage in an in-depth, all-consuming practice of news use. This requires, first, that news can be consumed without interruption or distraction, which can be facilitated online through on-demand and time-shifting availability, enabling a full-screen mode, and offering an ad-free experience option. It also requires that news is easy to save for later and easy to find back. Less intense, lean-back practices like *viewing* and *hearing* are facilitated by 24/7 supply and easy-to-find and accessible content, also available on demand and via time shifting. Though *glancing* is not a practice news organizations will typically want to focus on, it can be facilitated by extremely short messages (e.g. "Johnson out of hospital" on a screen in public transport).

For *checking*, it is imperative to have clear, descriptive headlines, listed chronologically and accompanied by time stamps to facilitate staying on top of the latest news. The news site or app must also be easy to navigate. The latter is also true for *scanning*, but here headlines should be accompanied by clear leads that facilitate quickly getting the gist of the story. On a news item level, this can also be facilitated through blocks with important quotes and summaries in the form of bullet points, in both digital and print. Bullet-point summaries also facilitate *reading* by functioning as a primer (these are the key points of the article worth focusing on), and quickly determining whether the article is worth *saving*. *Monitoring* involves a sense of urgency which makes the user want to actively stay on top of one event in order to act when necessary. This can be facilitated by continuous updates (e.g. in the form of a live blog) that highlight not only recency (through time stamps) but also importance. It is further facilitated by making it easy to "follow" this specific event, through push notifications or personalized sections of the news site or app (e.g. farmers may want to be continuously updated about nitrogen policies, and descendants of Turkish migrants about earthquakes in Turkey). Lean-back, easygoing digital practices of *snacking* and *scrolling* are facilitated by smoothly working sites and apps and a layout that makes it easy to slalom and to skip headlines, leads, images, and videos. Although content and form should always be platform appropriate, that is especially the case here: for example, texts and videos must be short and engaging on Facebook and Instagram; they must fit with the look and feel of the platform. It should be emphasized that these different, seemingly competing practices can also be facilitated at the same time. For instance, www.NRC.nl (the website of a quality Dutch newspaper) contains one block with chronologically ordered, time-stamped headlines that facilitate *checking*, in addition to a large section that includes headlines, succinct leads, and images that enable *scanning* and *snacking*. As mentioned in Chapter 4, this strategy maximizes not the number of clicks or the time that people spend on the story but the number of people that can appreciate the provided service.

Clicking demands informative headlines that contain the most important elements of the story. Here the need to know comes into play. What could be seen as positive clickbait is about synchronizing the importance of the news with the level of the bait: if journalists feel a story is crucial for their audience to know, this should be reflected in the headline's wording. This is also about helping the audience to find news that is important to them. *Saving* is facilitated by making it easy to save content (via clear buttons) as well as to find back the saved items. Since part of this practice is determining whether the content is worth saving and reading later, it can also be facilitated through easy navigation (e.g. quick scrolling) and clear, informative headings and bullet points (scanning).

Searching is facilitated by making it easy to find additional (background) information. This can be done through explainers and by making related content accessible through recommendations, dossiers, and user-friendly archives. It can also be facilitated through hyperlinks to own as well as others' content (easy to organize with affiliated news organizations) as well as taking on the role of a curator (recommendations for further reading, listening, or watching). Searching is further optimized by search engine optimization (SEO), making relevant content easily findable. *Triangulating* is facilitated in the same way as searching, with (due to its focus on truth-finding) the addition of source transparency, enabling users to check the validity and reliability of the news.

Avoiding news, which refers to skipping or slaloming around content users do not want to consume, requires easily recognizable genres, topics, and angles. When the avoidance is topic-based, personalization is an option, enabling users to (very easily) remove categories (e.g. sports) from their news overview. When the avoidance is valence based, news might be formulated in such a way that it does not (over)emphasize the negativity of the news when this is not warranted. News may also be brought through a constructive angle. *Abstaining* from news, which refers to (temporarily) teetotaling, can be facilitated by making it easy to turn off push notifications or by allowing subscribers to temporarily pause their subscription. Since abstaining is a spectrum, those who want to reduce the frequency of their news use can be served by offering a weekly briefing, such as a (paid) newsletter that contains the most important news of the week. Users who want to limit their news consumption to once a day may be asked when they want to receive their daily update.

Finally, all the "small acts of engagements" (Picone et al., 2019) – *commenting, linking, sharing, liking, recommending, tagging,* and *voting* – can be approached from a user perspective as "small acts of communication." The user wants to communicate something which can be facilitated by easy-to-find buttons, a broad range of emojis, and comment boxes.

Audience sensitivity as becoming attentive to the underlying logics of metrics

Second, audience sensitivity is about understanding the logics underlying different audience metrics and developing a particular *alertness* to properly deal with them. Although Chapters 3 and 4 critically explored the metrics, clicks, and time spent, our point is not that news organizations should not use them; indeed, metrics can provide significant information about what users find worth their while. What our results pointed against is taking metrics at face value: using clicks and time spent as a one-to-one reflection of interest, engagement, or attention. We showed that while clicks often do indicate some level of interest in news, sensational, "clickbaity" headlines seem to *incite* curiosity rather than reflect a *pre-existing* interest. In addition, user practices that are much appreciated by users (such as checking, scanning, snacking, and monitoring) may not register any clicks. As we explained extensively, lack of clicks should therefore not be confused with an absence of interest. What it may indicate instead is that users do not have to click in order be updated and feel sufficiently informed by the headlines. To take the COVID-19 crisis as an example: in March of 2020, when it was recognized by the World Health Organization (WHO) as a global pandemic, news about the virus skyrocketed, only to return to "normal" levels the following month (Benton, 2020). Although people may consume less news – and indeed, intentionally avoid news (Kalogeropoulos, Fletcher, & Nielsen, 2020) – our research suggests this does not necessarily mean a loss of interest. Instead – similar to our 2014 participants' reactions to news about the ongoing war in Syria, where they saw headlines indicating numbers of casualties as informative enough – clicking will not yield additional insights and may also unnecessarily bring them down. They do want to keep *seeing* the main headlines about the crisis, but they will only click once a truly new development happens or a new perspective is offered.

Being attentive, then, means becoming aware of the complexities and apparent paradoxes involved in metrics. This is also the case with time spent: while more attention minutes spent on a news item may point to an experience of appreciation, it can also reflect people being distracted and thus less engaged. In addition, less time spent on news may signify that the news item is easy to navigate and to make sense of, which is valuable to news users who want to scan to get a quick overview of what has happened.

Again, metrics – when used responsibly – *are* valuable for news organizations to understand their users. However, there is no one-size-fits-all approach to metrics: the appropriate (combination of) metrics for each news organization should be aligned with specific goals (Cherubini & Nielsen, 2016; see Groot Kormelink, 2019). For instance, clicks allow A/B testing to determine which (types of) headlines attract users to quality content. "Engaged time" and "scroll depth" can help journalists to see if users read their stories in full or where they dropped out. Social media click-through rates can help determine which content users find worth interrupting their flow scrolling (Chapter 5), whereas "session length" and "return visits" can help news organizations establish whether their audiences mostly engage in "reading," "checking," "scanning," or "snacking." Finally, conversion rates (via free trials, newsletters) can help gauge which (type of) content users find worth their money. For instance, Swedish newspaper *Dagens Nyheter* places articles behind a paywall if they hit a certain amount of traffic in their first hours; this strategy is good for 60% of their conversion rate (Southern, 2019).

Audience sensitivity as taking into account the affective and sensory dimensions of news use

The third articulation of audience sensitivity is paying more attention to the affective and sensory dimensions involved in news use. As Chapter 5 shows, since news is about more than cognition (selecting, informing, responding to news, etc.), becoming knowledgeable about other experiential dimensions is just as relevant for gaining insight into everyday use of news. While this book has focused less on how news *content* can affect people and how they value particular affective sensations (see Costera Meijer, 2021b; Groot Kormelink & Costera Meijer, 2017), Chapter 5 illustrates how people's affective states matter for the type and tone of news they seek out (and avoid) and appreciate. Familiarizing oneself with affective dimensions of news use is, we argue, about taking the emotions connected to the use of news seriously and making them *informative* and therefore *productive* for how journalists select, produce, and present news. For instance, at the start of the COVID-19 pandemic, Ann (59) sometimes felt so overwhelmed by the importance, relevance, and urgency of information that she had trouble taking it in: it was simply too much. She therefore was grateful for talk shows and newspapers that repeated the key information several times in different examples and with a broader range of tone of voice.

In terms of sensory experiences involved in news use, our results suggest that in addition to having smoothly working and intuitive designs, news organizations could help news users *master* their devices and interfaces. As Chapter 5 revealed, one obstacle for users to adopt news into their routines is lacking the practical and manual skills to efficiently handle and navigate (new) devices and platforms, as well as lacking the desire to put energy in acquiring this know-how. News organizations could make this process easier by offering accessible how-to guides to new users, such as a manual that explains the composition of the newspaper, website, or app so users know where to find relevant content, or in-app "directions" (e.g. "double-click to switch to full screen mode," "click here to save this article for later") (see Groot Kormelink, 2019).

How to deal with news user practices, preferences, and pleasures?

Becoming more sensitive toward people's changing news consumption practices and unchanged news experiences requires acquiring particular skills, developing an attitude of alertness, and becoming sufficiently knowledgeable about what changing news use means from a user perspective. This is a must for those news organizations and journalists who depend on audiences for their legitimation (public service media) or their business model. Since Berelson (1949) investigated what people missed during a newspaper strike, scholars and journalists have been aware of the broad spectrum of informative and ritual pleasures news consumers indulge in and rely upon to make it through the day. Nevertheless, the skills, alertness, and knowledge involved in becoming more sensitive to how people experience their (changing) news use are seldom at the top of the list of journalism educators.

If journalism wants to remain not only alive but also a constructive and vital force in democracies, news organizations, journalists, and journalism students should be prepared to take into consideration how they can provide a service that audiences truly appreciate. This book provides the basics of becoming more sensitive to changing news use, a sensitivity that demands new skills, new forms of alertness, and new types of knowledge.

References

Aalberg, T., Blekesaune, A., & Elvestad, E. (2013). Media choice and informed democracy. *International Journal of Press/Politics*, *18*(3), 281–303. https://doi.org/10.1177/1940161213485990

Anderson, C. (2011a). Between creative and quantified audiences: Web metrics and changing patterns of newswork in local US newsrooms. *Journalism: Theory, Practice & Criticism*, *12*(5), 550–566. https://doi.org/10.1177/1464884911402451

Anderson, C. (2011b). Deliberative, agonistic, and algorithmic audiences: Journalism's vision of its public in an age of audience transparency. *International Journal of Communication*, *5*, 529–547. http://ijoc.org/index.php/ijoc/article/view/884

Ang, I. (1991). *Desperately seeking the audience*. New York: Routledge.

Araujo, T., Wonneberger, A., Neijens, P., & de Vreese, C. (2017). How much time do you spend online? Understanding and improving the accuracy of self-reported measures of internet use. *Communication Methods and Measures*, *11*(3), 173–190. https://doi.org/10.1080/19312458.2017.1317337

Ashby, W. R. (1991). Requisite variety and its implications for the control of complex systems. In *Facets of systems science* (pp. 405–417). Boston: Springer.

Bakker, P. (2018). Het gaat prima met dagbladuitgevers (vooral met die van grote kranten). *Stimuleringsfonds voor de Journalistiek*. Retrieved from www.svdj.nl/nieuws/dagbladuitgevers-grote-kranten/

Bargas-Avila, J. A., & Hornbæk, K. (2011). Old wine in new bottles or novel challenges. *Proceedings of the 2011 annual conference on Human factors in computing systems - CHI '11*, 2689–2698. https://doi.org/10.1145/1978942.1979336

Bartsch, A., & Schneider, F. M. (2014). Entertainment and Politics Revisited: How Non-Escapist Forms of Entertainment Can Stimulate Political Interest and Information Seeking. *Journal of Communication 64*(3): 369–96.

Batsell, J. (2015). *Engaged journalism: Connecting with digitally empowered news audiences*. New York: Columbia University Press.

Bauwens, J., Thorbjornsson, G., & Verstrynge, K. (2019). Unplug your life: Digital detox through a Kierkegaardian Lens. *Kierkegaard Studies Yearbook*, *24*(1), 415–436. https://doi.org/10.1515/kierke-2019-0017

Belair-Gagnon, V., Zamith, R., & Holton, A. E. (2020). Role orientations and audience metrics in newsrooms: An examination of journalistic perceptions and their

drivers. *Digital Journalism*, *8*(3), 347–366. https://doi.org/10.1080/21670811.
2019.1709521

Benton, J. (2020). The coronavirus traffic bump to news sites is pretty much over already. *Nieman Lab*. Received from www.niemanlab.org/2020/04/the-coronavirus-traffic-bump-to-news-sites-is-pretty-much-over-already/

Berelson, B. (1949). What "missing the newspaper" means. In P. F. Lazarsfeld & F. N. Stanton (Eds.), *Communication research 1948–1949* (pp. 111–129). New York: Harper.

Bergström, A. (2008). The reluctant audience: Online participation in the Swedish journalistic context. *Westminster Papers in Communication and Culture*, *5*(2), 60. https://doi.org/10.16997/wpcc.67

Bird, S. E. (2011). Seeking the audience for news. Response, news talk, and everyday practices. In V. Nightingale (Ed.), *The handbook of media audiences* (pp. 489–508). Malden, MA: Wiley-Blackwell.

Blekesaune, A., Elvestad, E., & Aalberg, T. (2012). Tuning out the world of news and current affairs – an empirical study of Europe's disconnected citizens. *European Sociological Review*, *28*(1), 110–126. https://doi.org/10.1093/esr/jcq051

Bloor, M., Frankland, J., Thomas, M., & Stewart, K. (2001). *Focus Groups in Social Research (Introducing Qualitative Methods series)*. London: SAGE Publications Ltd.

Blumler, J. G., & Katz, E. (1974). *The uses of mass communications: Current perspectives on gratifications research*. Beverly Hills, CA: Sage.

Boczkowski, P. J., & Mitchelstein, E. (2010). Is there a gap between the news choices of journalists and consumers? A relational and dynamic approach. *International Journal of Press/Politics*, *15*(4), 420–440. https://doi.org/10.1177/1940161210374646

Boczkowski, P. J., & Mitchelstein, E. (2013). *The news gap: When the information preferences of the media and the public diverge*. Cambridge, MA: MIT Press.

Boczkowski, P. J., Mitchelstein, E., & Suenzo, F. (2020). The Smells, Sights, and Pleasures of Ink on Paper: The Consumption of Print Newspapers During a Period Marked by Their Crisis. *Journalism Studies*, *21*(5), 565–581. https://doi.org/10.1080/1461670x.2019.1670092

Bødker, H., & Sonnevend, J. (2018). The shifting temporalities of journalism: In memory of Kevin Barnhurst. *Journalism: Theory, Practice & Criticism*, *19*(1), 3–6. https://doi.org/10.1177/1464884916688510

Boesman, J., & Costera Meijer, I. (2018). "Don't read me the news, tell me the story": How news makers and storytellers differ in how they prepare and present stories. *Official Research Journal of the International Symposium on Online Journalism*, *8*(1), 13–32.

Booth, W. C., Colomb, G. G., & Williams, J. M. (2002). *The Craft of Research* (2nd ed.). London: The University of Chicago Press.

Brants, K., & de Haan, Y. (2010). Taking the public seriously: Three models of responsiveness in media and journalism. *Media, Culture & Society*, *32*(3), 411–428. https://doi.org/10.1177/0163443709361170

Brennen, B. (2019). *Opting out of digital media*. Oxford: Routledge.

Bruce, C. S., Davis, K., Hughes, H., Partridge, H. L., & Stoodley, I. (2014). *Information experience: Approaches to theory and practice*. Bingley, UK: Emerald Group Publishing Ltd.

Bryant, A., & Charmaz, K. (2007). *The SAGE Handbook of Grounded Theory*. Thousand Oaks, Canada: SAGE Publications.

Cammaerts, B., & Couldry, N. (2016). Digital journalism as practice. In T. Witschge, C. Anderson, D. Domingo, & A. Hermida (Eds.), *The Sage handbook of digital journalism* (pp. 326–340). London: Sage.

Carlson, M., & Lewis, S. C. (2018). Temporal reflexivity in journalism studies: Making sense of change in a more timely fashion. *Journalism, 20*(5), 642–650. https://doi.org/10.1177/1464884918760675

Charmaz, K. (2006). *Constructing grounded theory: A practical guide through qualitative analysis*. Thousand Oaks, CA: Sage.

Cherubini, F., & Nielsen, R. K. (2016). Editorial analytics: How news media are developing and using audience data and metrics. *Reuters Institute for the Study of Journalism*. Received from https://reutersinstitute.politics.ox.ac.uk/our-research/editorial-analytics-how-news-media-are-developing-and-using-audience-data-and-metrics

Christensen, C., Skok, D., & Allworth, J. (2012). Breaking news. Mastering the art of disruptive innovation in journalism. *Nieman Reports, 66*(3), 6–20.

Christin, A. (2014). When it comes to chasing clicks, journalists say one thing but feel pressure to do another. *NiemanLab*. Received from www.niemanlab.org/2014/08/when-it-comes-to-chasing-clicks-journalists-say-one-thing-but-feel-pressure-to-do-another/

Chyi, H. I., & Ng, Y. M. M. (2020). Still unwilling to pay: An empirical analysis of 50 U.S. newspapers' digital subscription results. *Digital Journalism*, 1–22. https://doi.org/10.1080/21670811.2020.1732831

Coddington, M. (2015). Clarifying journalism's quantitative turn. *Digital Journalism, 3*(3), 331–348. https://doi.org/10.1080/21670811.2014.976400

Cohen, N. S. (2019). At work in the digital newsroom. *Digital Journalism, 7*(5), 571–591. https://doi.org/10.1080/21670811.2017.1419821

Cook, J. (2011). Listening for listeners. The work of arranging how listening will occur in cultures of recorded sound. In V. Nightingale (Ed.), *The Handbook of media audiences* (pp. 41–61). Malden, MA: Wiley-Blackwell.

Corbin, J. M., & Strauss, A. (1990). Grounded theory research: Procedures, canons, and evaluative criteria. *Qualitative Sociology, 13*(1), 3–21. https://doi.org/10.1007/bf00988593

Cornia, A., Sehl, A., & Nielsen, R. K. (2020). "We no longer live in a time of separation": A comparative analysis of how editorial and commercial integration became a norm. *Journalism, 21*(2), 172–190. https://doi.org/10.1177/1464884918779919

Costera Meijer, I. (2001). The public quality of popular journalism: Developing a normative framework. *Journalism Studies, 2*(2), 189–205. https://doi.org/10.1080/14616700120042079

Costera Meijer, I. (2003). What is quality television news? A plea for extending the professional repertoire of newsmakers. *Journalism Studies, 4*(1): 15–29.

Costera Meijer, I. (2006). *De toekomst van het nieuws*. Amsterdam: Otto Cramwinckel.

Costera Meijer, I. (2007). The paradox of popularity. *Journalism Studies*, *8*(1), 96–116. https://doi.org/10.1080/14616700601056874

Costera Meijer, I. (2008). Checking, snacking and bodysnatching. How young people use the news and implications for public service media journalism. In G. F. Lowe & J. Bardoel (Eds.), *From public service broadcasting to public service media (RIPE@2007)* (pp. 167–186). Göteborg: Nordicom.

Costera Meijer, I. (2013). Valuable journalism: A search for quality from the vantage point of the user. *Journalism: Theory, Practice & Criticism*, *14*(6), 754–770. https://doi.org/10.1177/1464884912455899

Costera Meijer, I. (2016). Practicing audience-centred journalism research. In T. Witschge, C. Anderson, D. Domingo, A. Hermida (Eds.), *The Sage handbook of digital journalism* (pp. 546–561). London: Sage.

Costera Meijer, I. (2020a). Journalism, audiences and news experience. In K. Wahl-Jorgensen & T. Hanitzsch (Eds.), *The handbook of journalism studies* (2nd ed., pp. 730–761). London: Routledge.

Costera Meijer, I. (2020b). What does the audience experience as valuable local journalism? Approaching local news quality from a user's perspective. In A. Gulyas & D. Baines (Eds.), *The Routledge companion to local media and journalism* (pp. 357–367). London: Routledge.

Costera Meijer, I. (2021a). Understanding the audience turn in journalism. Forthcoming.

Costera Meijer, I. (2021b). What is valuable journalism? Forthcoming.

Costera Meijer, I., & Groot Kormelink, T. (2016). Revisiting the audience turn in journalism: How a user-based approach changes the meaning of clicks, transparency and citizen participation. In B. Franklin & S. Eldridge II. (Eds.), *The Routledge companion to digital journalism studies* (pp. 345–353). Oxford: Routledge.

Couldry, N. (2004). Theorising media as practice. *Social Semiotics*, *14*(2), 115–132. https://doi.org/10.1080/1035033042000238295

Couldry, N. (2011). The necessary future of the audience . . . and how to research it. In V. Nightingale (Ed.), *The handbook of media audiences* (pp. 213–229). Malden, MA: Wiley-Blackwell.

Couldry, N. (2012). *Media, society, world: Social theory and digital media practice*. Cambridge: Polity Press.

Couldry, N., & Markham, T. (2008). Troubled closeness or satisfied distance? Researching media consumption and public orientation. *Media, Culture & Society*, *30*(1), 5–21. https://doi.org/10.1177/0163443707084347

Courtois, C., Verdegem, P., & De Marez, L. (2013). The triple articulation of media technologies in audiovisual media consumption. *Television & New Media*, *14*(5), 421–439. https://doi.org/10.1177/1527476412439106

Dahlgren, P., & Sparks, C. (1992). *Journalism and Popular Culture*. London: SAGE

Darnton, R. (1975). Writing news and telling stories. *Daedalus*, *104*(2), 175–194. http://nrs.harvard.edu/urn-3:HUL.InstRepos:3403047

Davenport, T. H., & Beck, J. C. (2001). *The attention economy: Understanding the new currency of business*. Cambridge, MA: Harvard Business Press.

Davis, J. L., & Chouinard, J. B. (2016). Theorizing affordances: From request to refuse. *Bulletin of Science, Technology & Society, 36*(4), 241–248. https://doi.org/10.1177/0270467617714944

del Rio Carral, M. (2014). Focusing on "a day in the life": An activity-based method for the qualitative analysis of psychological phenomena. *Qualitative Research in Psychology, 11*(3), 298–315. https://doi.org/10.1080/14780887.2014.902525

Denzin, N. K. (1978). *The research act*. Chicago, IL: Aldine.

Deuze, M. (2011). Media life. *Media, Culture & Society, 33*(1), 137–148. https://doi.org/10.1177/0163443710386518

D'heer, E., Paulussen, S., & Courtois, C. (2012). Meerdere schermen in de huiskamer: een onderzoek naar simultaan mediagebruik. *Tijdschrift voor Communicatiewetenschap, 40*(4), 60–70. http://hdl.handle.net/1854/LU-3083986

Dimmick, J., Feaster, J. C., & Hoplamazian, G. J. (2011). News in the interstices: The niches of mobile media in space and time. *New Media & Society, 13*(1), 23–39. https://doi.org/10.1177/1461444810363452

Doeve, M., & Costera Meijer, I. (2013). *The value of transparency in journalism for audiences and (public) media organizations*. Paper presented at the Future of Journalism Conference, Cardiff, September 12–13.

Domingo, D., Masip, P., & Costera Meijer, I. (2015). Tracing digital news networks. *Digital Journalism, 3*(1), 53–67. https://doi.org/10.1080/21670811.2014.927996

Dongen van, M. (2020, April 22). Onstilbaar: Kwaliteitskranten in crisistijd. *De Volkskrant*.

Donsbach, W. (1991). Exposure to political content in newspapers: The impact of cognitive dissonance on readers' selectivity. *European Journal of Communication, 6*(2), 155–186. https://doi.org/10.1177/0267323191006002003

Drok, N., & Hermans, L. (2016). Is there a future for slow journalism? *Journalism Practice, 10*(4), 539–554. https://doi.org/10.1080/17512786.2015.1102604

Duffy, A., & Ling, R. (2020). The Gift of News: Phatic News Sharing on Social Media for Social Cohesion. *Journalism Studies, 21*(1), 72–87. https://doi.org/10.1080/1461670x.2019.1627900

Edgerly, S., Mourão, R. R., Thorson, E., & Tham, S. M. (2020). When do audiences verify? How perceptions about message and source influence audience verification of news headlines. *Journalism & Mass Communication Quarterly, 97*(1), 52–71. https://doi.org/10.1177/1077699019864680

Edgerly, S., Thorson, K., Thorson, E., Vraga, E. K., & Bode, L. (2018). Do parents still model news consumption? Socializing news use among adolescents in a multi-device world. *New Media & Society, 20*(4), 1263–1281. https://doi.org/10.1177/1461444816688451

Edgerly, S., & Vraga, E. K. (2019). News, entertainment, or both? Exploring audience perceptions of media genre in a hybrid media environment. *Journalism, 20*(6), 807–826. https://doi.org/10.1177/1464884917730709

Elvestad, E., & Shaker, L. (2017). Media choice proliferation and shifting orientations towards news in the United States and Norway, 1995–2012. *Nordicom Review, 38*(2), 33–49. https://doi.org/10.1515/nor-2016-0390

Ericsson, K. A., & Simon, H. A. (1993). *Protocol analysis: Verbal reports as data* (Rev. ed.). Cambridge, MA: Bradford Books/MIT Press.

Fortunati, L., Taipale, S., & Farinosi, M. (2015). Print and online newspapers as material artefacts. *Journalism: Theory, Practice & Criticism*, *16*(6), 830–846. https://doi.org/10.1177/1464884914545439

Gallagher, K. P., Kaiser, K. M., Simon, J. C., Beath, C. M., & Goles, T. (2010). The requisite variety of skills for IT professionals. *Communications of the ACM*, *53*(6), 144–148. https://doi.org/10.1145/1743546.1743584

Galtung, J., & Ruge, M. H. (1965). The structure of foreign news. *Journal of Peace Research*, *2*(1), 64–90. https://doi.org/10.1177/002234336500200104

Gans, H. J. (1979). *Deciding what's news*. Chicago, IL: Northwestern University Press.

Gauntlett, D. (2007). *Creative explorations. New approaches to identities and audiences*. London: Routledge.

Gauntlett, D. (2011). *Making is connecting: The social meaning of creativity, from DIY and knitting to YouTube and Web 2.0*. Cambridge: Polity Press.

Giddens, A. (1991). *Modernity and self-identity. Self and society in the late modern age*. Cambridge: Polity Press.

Glasser, T. L. (2000). The Politics of Public Journalism. *Journalism Studies*, *1*(4), 683–686. https://doi.org/10.1080/146167000441385

Golding, P., & Elliott, P. (1979). *Making the news*. London: Longman.

Goyanes, M., Demeter, M., & de Grado, L. (2020). The culture of free: Construct explication and democratic ramifications for readers' willingness to pay for public affairs news. *Journalism*, 1–17. https://doi.org/10.1177/1464884920913436

Grabe, M. E., Lang, A., & Zhao, X. (2003). News Content and Form. *Communication Research*, *30*(4), 387–413. https://doi.org/10.1177/0093650203253368

Grabe, M. E., Zhou, S., Lang, A., & Bolls, P. D. (2000). Packaging Television News: The Effects of Tabloid on Information Processing and Evaluative Responses. *Journal of Broadcasting & Electronic Media*, *44*(4), 581–598. https://doi.org/10.1207/s15506878jobem4404_4

Green, M. C., & Brock, T. C. (2000). The Role of Transportation in the Persuasiveness of Public Narratives. *Journal of Personality and Social Psychology 79*(5): 701–21.

Groot Kormelink, T. (2019). *Capturing and making sense of everyday news use* (PhD thesis). Vrije Universiteit Amsterdam, Amsterdam.

Groot Kormelink, T. (2020). Seeing, thinking, feeling: A critical reflection on interview-based methods for studying news use. *Journalism Studies*, *21*(7), 863–878. https://doi.org/10.1080/1461670x.2020.1716829

Groot Kormelink, T., & Costera Meijer, I. (2014). Tailor-made news. *Journalism Studies*, *15*(5), 632–641. https://doi.org/10.1080/1461670x.2014.894367

Groot Kormelink, T., & Costera Meijer, I. (2017). It's catchy, but it gets you f*cking nowhere. *International Journal of Press/Politics*, *22*(2), 143–162. https://doi.org/10.1177/1940161217690881

de Haan, Y. M. (2012). *Between professional autonomy and public responsibility: accountability and responsiveness in Dutch media and journalism* (PhD thesis). University of Amsterdam, Amsterdam.

Hall, S. (1973). *Encoding and decoding in the media discourse.* Stencilled paper no. 7, Centre for Contemporary Cultural Studies, University of Birmingham, Birmingham.

Hanusch, F. (2017). Web analytics and the functional differentiation of journalism cultures: Individual, organizational and platform-specific influences on news-work. *Information, Communication & Society, 20*(10), 1571–1586. https://doi.org/10.1080/1369118x.2016.1241294

Harambam, J., Helberger, N., & van Hoboken, J. (2018). Democratizing algorithmic news recommenders: How to materialize voice in a technologically saturated media ecosystem. *Philosophical Transactions of the Royal Society A, 376*, 1–21. https://doi.org/10.1098/rsta.2018.0088

Harcup, T., & O'Neill, D. (2001). What is news? Galtung and Ruge revisited. *Journalism Studies, 2*(2), 261–280. https://doi.org/10.1080/14616700118449

Hasebrink, U. & Popp, J. (2006). Media repertoires as a result of selective media use: A conceptual approach to the analysis of patterns of exposure. *Communications: The European Journal of Communication Research, 31*(3): 369–387.

Hassenzahl, M., & Tractinsky, N. (2006). User experience - a research agenda. *Behaviour & Information Technology, 25*(2), 91–97. https://doi.org/10.1080/01449290500330331

Hatcher, J., & Haavik, E. (2014). We write with our hearts. *Journalism Practice, 8*(2), 149–163. https://doi.org/10.1080/17512786.2013.859828

Hendriks Vettehen, P. G. J., Nuijten, K., & Peeters, A. (2008). Explaining Effects of Sensationalism on Liking of Television News Stories. *Communication Research, 35*(3), 319–338. https://doi.org/10.1177/0093650208315960

Hermes, J. (1995). *Reading women's magazines. An analysis of everyday media use.* Cambridge: Polity Press.

Hermida, A., Fletcher, F., Korell, D., & Logan, D. (2012). Share, like, recommend. *Journalism Studies, 13*(5–6), 815–824. https://doi.org/10.1080/1461670x.2012.664430

Hersh, E. (2020). *Politics is for power: How to move beyond political hobbyism, take action, and make real change.* New York: Scribner.

Het Parool. (2017, June 22) "Vier op de tien Nederlanders kijkt of leest nauwelijks het nieuws." *Het Parool.* Retreived from https://www.parool.nl/kunst-en-media/vier-op-de-tien-nederlanders-kijkt-of-leest-nauwelijks-het-nieuws~a4502073/

Holstein, J.A., & Gubrium, J. F. (2003). *Postmodern interviewing.* Thousand Oaks, CA: Sage.

Hoplamazian, G.J., Dimmick, J., Ramirez, A., Jr., & Feaster, J. (2018). Capturing mobility: The time – space diary as a method for assessing media use niches. *Mobile Media & Communication, 6*(1), 127–145. https://doi.org/10.1177/2050157917731484

Ihde, D. (1990). *Technology and the lifeworld: From garden to earth.* Bloomington: Indiana University Press.

Ihde, D. (2008). Introduction: Postphenomenological research. *Human Studies, 31*(1), 1–9. https://doi.org/10.1007/s10746-007-9077-2

Ingold, T. (2000). *The perception of the environment: Essays on livelihood, dwelling and skill*. London: Routledge.

Ingold, T. (2011). *Being alive: Essays on movement, knowledge and description*. London: Routledge.

Kalogeropoulos, A., Fletcher, R., & Nielsen, R. K. (2018). News brand attribution in distributed environments: Do people know where they get their news? *New Media & Society, 21*(3), 583–601. https://doi.org/10.1177/1461444818801313

Kalogeropoulos, A., Fletcher, R., & Nielsen, R. K. (2020). Initial surge in news use around coronavirus in the UK has been followed by significant increase in news avoidance. Reuters institute for the study of journalism. *Reuters Institute for the Study of Journalism*. Retrieved from https://reutersinstitute.politics.ox.ac. uk/initial-surge-news-use-around-coronavirus-uk-has-been-followed-significant-increase-news-avoidance

Karlsson, M., & Clerwall, C. (2013). Negotiating professional news judgment and "clicks." *Nordicom Review, 34*(2), 65–76. https://doi.org/10.2478/nor-2013-0054

Katz, E., Gurevitch, M., & Haas, H. (1973). On the use of the mass media for important things. *American Sociological Review, 38*(2), 164–181. Retrieved from https://repository.upenn.edu/asc_papers/267

Keightley, E. (2013). From immediacy to intermediacy: The mediation of lived time. *Time & Society, 22*(1), 55–75. https://doi.org/10.1177/0961463x11402045

Keightley, E., & Downey, J. (2018). The intermediate time of news consumption. *Journalism: Theory, Practice & Criticism, 19*(1), 93–110. https://doi.org/10.1177/1464884916689155

Kleppe, M., & Costera Meijer, I. (2015). *Tracking digitally consumed news: Monitoring and understanding everyday online news consumption of young highly-educated students*. Presented at the Future of Journalism Conference, Cardiff, September 24–26.

Kleppe, M., & Otte, M. (2017). Analysing and understanding news consumption patterns by tracking online user behaviour with a multimodal research design. *Digital Scholarship in the Humanities, 32*(suppl. 2), ii158–ii170. https://doi.org/10.1093/llc/fqx030

Kruikemeier, S., Lecheler, S., & Boyer, M. M. (2018). Learning from news on different media platforms: An eye-tracking experiment. *Political Communication, 35*(1), 75–96. https://doi.org/10.1080/10584609.2017.1388310

Ksiazek, T. B., Malthouse, E. C., & Webster, J. G. (2010). News-seekers and Avoiders: Exploring Patterns of Total News Consumption Across Media and the Relationship to Civic Participation. *Journal of Broadcasting & Electronic Media, 54*(4), 551–568. https://doi.org/10.1080/08838151.2010.519808

Kuiken, J., Schuth, A., Spitters, M., & Marx, M. (2017). Effective headlines of newspaper articles in a digital environment. *Digital Journalism, 5*(10), 1300–1314. https://doi.org/10.1080/21670811.2017.1279978

Kümpel, A. S. (2020). The Matthew effect in social media news use: Assessing inequalities in news exposure and news engagement on social network sites (SNS). *Journalism*, 1–16. https://doi.org/10.1177/1464884920915374

Lagerwerf, L., & Verheij, D. (2014). Hypertext in online news stories. *Information Design Journal*, *21*(2), 163–178. https://doi.org/10.1075/idj.21.2.07lag

Lahlou, S. (2011). How can we capture the subject's perspective? An evidence-based approach for the social scientist. *Social Science Information*, *50*(3–4), 607–655. https://doi.org/10.1177/0539018411411033

Lang, A., Shin, M., Bradley, S. D., Wang, Z., Lee, S., & Potter, D. (2005). Wait! Don't Turn That Dial! More Excitement to Come! The Effects of Story Length and Production Pacing in Local Television News on Channel Changing Behavior and Information Processing in a Free Choice Environment. *Journal of Broadcasting & Electronic Media*, *49*(1), 3–22. https://doi.org/10.1207/s15506878jobem4901_2

Larsen, B. S. (2000). Radio as ritual. An approach to everyday use of radio. *Nordicom Review*, *2*, 259–275.

Larsson, A. O. (2018). The News User on Social Media. *Journalism Studies*, *19*(15), 2225–2242. https://doi.org/10.1080/1461670x.2017.1332957

Latour, B. (2005). *Reassembling the Social: An Introduction to Actor-network-theory*. New York: Oxford University Press.

Lee, A. M., Lewis, S. C., & Powers, M. (2014). Audience clicks and news placement. *Communication Research*, *41*(4), 505–530. https://doi.org/10.1177/0093650212467031

Le Masurier, M. (2015). What is slow journalism? *Journalism Practice*, *9*(2), 138–152. https://doi.org/10.1080/17512786.2014.916471

Lewis, J., Inthorn, S., & Wahl-Jorgensen, K. (2005). *Citizens or consumers? What the media tell us about political participation*. Buckingham: Open University Press.

Lindlof, T. R. (1995). Eliciting experience: Interviews. In *Qualitative communication research methods* (pp. 163–194). Thousand Oaks, CA: Sage.

List, D. (2004). Maximum variation sampling for surveys and consensus groups. *Audience Dialogue*. Retrieved from www.audiencedialogue.org/maxvar.html

Lull, J. (1990). *Inside family viewing: Ethnographic research on television's audiences*. London: Routledge.

MacGregor, P. (2007). Tracking the online audience. *Journalism Studies*, *8*(2), 280–298. https://doi.org/10.1080/14616700601148879

Madianou, M. (2009). Audience reception and news in everyday life. In K. Wahl-Jorgensen & T. Hanitzsch (Eds.), *The handbook of journalism studies* (pp. 325–337). New York: Routledge.

Madianou, M. (2010). Living with news: Ethnographies of news consumption. In S. Allan (Ed.), *The Routledge companion to news and journalism* (pp. 428–438). London: Routledge.

Mangen, A. (2008). Hypertext fiction reading: Haptics and immersion. *Journal of Research in Reading*, *31*(4), 404–419. https://doi.org/10.1111/j.1467-9817.2008.00380.x

McDonagh, D., Bruseberg, A., & Haslam, C. (2002). Visual product evaluation: Exploring users' emotional relationships with products. *Applied Ergonomics*, *33*(3), 231–240. https://doi.org/10.1016/s0003-6870(02)00008-x

Merleau-Ponty, M. (1962). *Phenomenology of perception*. London: Routledge and Kegan Paul.

Miller, V. (2008). New media, networking and phatic culture. *Convergence: The International Journal of Research into New Media Technologies*, *14*(4), 387–400. https://doi.org/10.1177/1354856508094659

Mindich, D.T.Z. (2005). *Tuned out: Why Americans under 40 don't follow the news.* New York: Oxford University Press.

Moeller, S.D. (1999). *Compassion fatigue: How the media sell disease, famine, war, and death.* New York: Routledge.

Molyneux, L. (2018). Mobile news consumption. *Digital Journalism*, *6*(5), 634–650. https://doi.org/10.1080/21670811.2017.1334567

Moores, S. (2012). *Media, place and mobility.* Basingstoke: Palgrave Macmillan.

Moores, S. (2015). We find our way about: Everyday media use and "inhabitant knowledge." *Mobilities*, *10*(1), 17–35. https://doi.org/10.1080/17450101.2013.8 19624

Moores, S. (2014). Digital orientations: "Ways of the hand" and practical knowing in media uses and other manual activities. *Mobile Media & Communication*, *2*(2), 196–208. https://doi.org/10.1177/2050157914521091

Myllylahti, M. (2019). Paying attention to attention: A conceptual framework for studying news reader revenue models related to platforms. *Digital Journalism*, 1–9. https://doi.org/10.1080/21670811.2019.1691926

Napoli, P.M. (2011). *Audience evolution: New technologies and the transformation of media audiences.* New York: Columbia University Press.

Neijens, P.C., & Voorveld, H.A. (2016). Digital replica editions versus printed newspapers: Different reading styles? Different recall? *New Media & Society*, *20*(2), 760–776. https://doi.org/10.1177/1461444816670326

Nelson, J.L., & Lei, R.F. (2018). The effect of digital platforms on news audience behavior. *Digital Journalism*, *6*(5), 619–633. https://doi.org/10.1080/21670811. 2017.1394202

Nelson, J. L., & Tandoc Jr., E. C. (2019). Doing "Well" or Doing "Good": What Audience Analytics Reveal About Journalism's Competing Goals. *Journalism Studies*, *20*(13), 1960–1976. https://doi.org/10.1080/1461670x.2018.1547122

Nelson, J.L., & Webster, J.G. (2016). Audience currencies in the age of big data. *International Journal on Media Management*, *18*(1), 9–24. https://doi.org/10.1080/14241277.2016.1166430

Neverla, I., & Trümper, S. (2019). As time goes by: Tracking polychronic temporalities in journalism and mediated memory. *Mediated Time*, 219–237. https://doi.org/10.1007/978-3-030-24950-2_11

Newman, N. (2016). News alerts and the battle for the lockscreen. *Reuters Institute for the Study of Journalism.* Retrieved from https://reutersinstitute.politics.ox.ac.uk/sites/default/files/research/files/News%2520Alerts%2520and%2520the%2520 Battle%2520for%2520the%2520Lockscreen.pdf

Newman, N., Fletcher, R., Kalogeropoulos, A., Levy, D., & Nielsen, R.K. (2018). Reuters institute digital news report 2018. *Reuters Institute for the Study of Journalism.* Retrieved from http://media.digitalnewsreport.org/wp-content/uploads/2018/06/digital-news-report-2018.pdf

Newman, N., Fletcher, R., Kalogeropoulos, A., & Nielsen, R.K. (2019). Reuters institute digital news report 2019. *Reuters Institute for the Study of Journalism.*

Retrieved from https://reutersinstitute.politics.ox.ac.uk/sites/default/files/inline-files/DNR_2019_FINAL.pdf

Newman, N., Fletcher, R., Levy, D.A.L., & Nielsen, R. K. (2016). Reuters institute digital news report 2016. *Reuters Institute for the Study of Journalism*. Retrieved from http://reutersinstitute.politics.ox.ac.uk/sites/default/files/Digital-News-Report-2016.pdf

Newman, N., Fletcher, R., Schulz, A., Andı, S., & Nielsen, R. K. (2020). Reuters institute digital news report 2020. *Reuters Institute for the Study of Journalism*. Retrieved from https://reutersinstitute.politics.ox.ac.uk/sites/default/files/2020-06/DNR_2020_FINAL.pdf

Nguyen, A. (2013). Online news audiences: The challenges of web metrics. In S. Allan & K. Fowler-Watt (Eds.), *Journalism: New challenges* (pp. 146–161). Poole: CJCR: Centre for Journalism & Communication Research, Bournemouth University.

Nielsen, R.K. (2019). Foreword. In N. Newman, R. Fletcher, A. Kalogeropoulos, & R.K. Nielsen (Eds.), *Reuters institute digital news report 2019*. Oxford: Reuters Institute for the Study of Journalism.

Nielsen, R.K., & Graves, L. (2017). What do ordinary people think fake news is? Poor journalism and political propaganda. *Columbia Journalism Review*. Retrieved from www.cjr.org/analysis/fake-news-study.php

Nieuwsmonitor. (2013). Seksmoord op horrorvakantie: De invloed van bezoekersgedrag op krantenwebsites op de nieuwsselectie van dagbladen en hun websites. *De Nederlandse Nieuwsmonitor*. Retrieved from www.nieuwsmonitor.net/d/244/Seksmoord_op_Horrorvakantie_pdf

Obbink, H. (2017, June 22) "Vier op de tien Nederlanders lezen of kijken nauwelijks nieuws." *Trouw*. Retrieved from https://www.trouw.nl/samenleving/vier-op-de-tien-nederlanders-leest-of-kijkt-nauwelijks-nieuws~a1507d2c/.

O'Brien, H.L., Freund, L., & Westman, S. (2014). What motivates the online news browser? News item selection in a social information seeking scenario. *Information Research, 19*(3). Retrieved from www.informationr.net/ir/19-3/paper634.html

Oeldorf-Hirsch, A., & Sundar, S. S. (2015). Posting, commenting, and tagging: Effects of sharing news stories on Facebook. *Computers in Human Behavior, 44*, 240–249. https://doi.org/10.1016/j.chb.2014.11.024

Oliver, M. B., & Bartsch, A. (2010). Appreciation as Audience Response: Exploring Entertainment Gratifications beyond Hedonism. *Human Communication Research 36*(1): 53–81.

O'Neill, D., & Harcup, T. (2009). News values and selectivity. In K. Wahl-Jorgensen & T. Hanitzsch (Eds.), *The handbook of journalism studies* (pp. 161–174). London: Routledge.

Parisi, D., Paterson, M., & Archer, J. E. (2017). Haptic media studies. *New Media & Society, 19*(10), 1513–1522. https://doi.org/10.1177/1461444817717518

Park, C. S. (2019). Does too much news on social media discourage news seeking? Mediating role of news efficacy between perceived news overload and news avoidance on social media. *Social Media + Society, 5*(3), 1–12. https://doi.org/10.1177/2056305119872956

Patton, M. Q. (1990). *Qualitative evaluation and research methods*. Thousand Oaks, CA: Sage.

Perks, L. G., & Turner, J. S. (2019). Podcasts and Productivity: A Qualitative Uses and Gratifications Study. *Mass Communication and Society*, *22*(1), 96–116. https://doi.org/10.1080/15205436.2018.1490434

Peters, C. (2012). Journalism to go. *Journalism Studies*, *13*(5–6), 695–705. https://doi.org/10.1080/1461670x.2012.662405

Peters, C. (2016). The spatiotemporal dynamics of digital news audiences. In B. Franklin & S. Eldridge II (Eds.), *The Routledge companion to digital journalism studies* (pp. 375–384). London: Routledge.

Peters, C., & Schrøder, K. C. (2018). Beyond the here and now of news audiences: A process-based framework for investigating news repertoires. *Journal of Communication*, *68*(6), 1079–1103. https://doi.org/10.1093/joc/jqy060

Picone, I. (2011). Produsage as a form of self-publication. A qualitative study of casual news produsage. *New Review of Hypermedia and Multimedia*, *17*(1), 99–120. https://doi.org/10.1080/13614568.2011.552643

Picone, I., Kleut, J., Pavlíčková, T., Romic, B., Møller Hartley, J., & De Ridder, S. (2019). Small acts of engagement: Reconnecting productive audience practices with everyday agency. *New Media & Society*, *21*(9), 2010–2028. https://doi.org/10.1177/1461444819837569

Pink, S. (2009). *Doing sensory ethnography*. London: Sage.

Pink, S. (2012). *Situating everyday life: Practices and places*. London: Sage.

Pink, S. (2015). Approaching media through the senses: Between experience and representation. *Media International Australia*, *154*(1), 5–14. https://doi.org/10.1177/1329878x1515400103

Pink, S., & Leder Mackley, K. (2013). Saturated and situated: Expanding the meaning of media in the routines of everyday life. *Media, Culture & Society*, *35*(6), 677–691. https://doi.org/10.1177/0163443713491298

Potter, J., & Hepburn, A. (2005). Qualitative interviews in psychology: Problems and possibilities. *Qualitative Research in Psychology*, *2*(4), 281–307. https://doi.org/10.1191/1478088705qp045oa

Potter, J., & Wetherell, M. (1987). *Discourse and social psychology: Beyond attitudes and behaviour*. London: Sage.

Prior, M. (2009). The immensely inflated news audience: Assessing bias in self-reported news exposure. *Public Opinion Quarterly*, *73*(1), 130–143. https://doi.org/10.1093/poq/nfp002

Purcell, K., Rainie, L., Mitchell, A., Rosenstiel, T., & Olmstead, K. (2010). Understanding the participatory news consumer: How internet and cell phone users have turned news into a social experience. *Pew Research Center*. Retrieved from www.pewinternet.org/files/old-media//Files/Reports/2010/PIP_Understanding_the_Participatory_News_Consumer.pdf

Richardson, I., & Hjorth, L. (2017). Mobile media, domestic play and haptic ethnography. *New Media & Society*, *19*(10), 1653–1667. https://doi.org/10.1177/1461444817717516

Roth, F. S., Weinmann, C., Schneider, F. M., Hopp, F. R., & Vorderer, P. (2014). Seriously Entertained: Antecedents and Consequences of Hedonic and Eudaimonic Entertainment Experiences With Political Talk Shows on TV. *Mass Communication and Society*, *17*(3), 379–399. https://doi.org/10.1080/15205436.2014.891135

Rothbart, M. & Taylor, M. (1992). Category labels and social reality: Do we view social categories as natural kinds? In G. R. Semin & K. Fiedler (Eds.), *Language, interaction, and social cognition* (pp. 11–36). Thousand Oaks, CA: Sage.

Rosenberger, R., & Verbeek, P. P. (2015). A field guide to postphenomenology. In R. Rosenberger & P. P. Verbeek (Eds.), *Postphenomenological investigations: Essays on human-technology relations* (pp. 9–41). London: Lexington Books.

Rosenstiel, T. (2013). *Where are news audiences taking journalism?* Retrieved from www.youtube.com/watch?v=NngL2-5FFy4&feature=player_detailpage

Ruggiero, T. E. (2000). Uses and gratifications theory in the 21st century. *Mass Communication and Society, 3*(1), 3–37. https://doi.org/10.1207/s15327825 mcs0301_02

Schaudt, S., & Carpenter, S. (2009). The news that's fit to click: An analysis of online news values and preferences present in the most-viewed stories on azcentral.com. *Southwestern Mass Communication Journal, 24*(2), 17–26.

Schlesinger, P. (1978). *Putting "reality" together*. Beverly Hills, CA: Sage.

Schrøder, K. C. (2015). News media old and new. *Journalism Studies, 16*(1), 60–78. https://doi.org/10.1080/1461670x.2014.890332

Schrøder, K. C., & Steeg Larsen, B. (2010). The shifting cross-media news landscape. *Journalism Studies, 11*(4), 524–534. https://doi.org/10.1080/1461670100 3638392

Schudson, M. (1998). *The good citizen: A history of American civic life*. Cambridge, MA: Harvard University Press.

Scire, S. (2020, April 6). For its must-read coronavirus coverage, the *Atlantic* is rewarded with a huge surge of digital subscriptions. *Nieman Lab*. Retrieved from www.niemanlab.org/2020/04/for-its-must-read-coronavirus-coverage-the-atlantic-is-rewarded-with-a-huge-surge-of-digital-subscriptions/

SCP.nl. (2017). Klassieke media nog dominant bij nieuwsgebruik. *SCP*. Retrieved from www.scp.nl/Nieuws/Klassieke_media_nog_dominant_bij_nieuwsgebruik

Seamon, D. (1979). *A geography of the lifeworld: Movement, rest and encounter*. London: Croom Helm Ltd.

Segijn, C. M., Voorveld, H. A. M., & Smit, E. G. (2016). The underlying mechanisms of multi-screening effects. *Journal of Advertising, 45*(4), 391–402. https://doi.org /10.1080/00913367.2016.1172386

Silverstone, R. (1994). *Television and everyday life*. London: Routledge.

Skovsgaard, M., & Andersen, K. (2020). Conceptualizing News Avoidance: Towards a Shared Understanding of Different Causes and Potential Solutions. *Journalism Studies, 21*(4), 459–476. https://doi.org/10.1080/1461670x.2019.1686410

Southern, L. (2019, May 20). How Swedish newspaper Dagens Nyheter halved subscriber churn in 2 years. *Digiday*. Retrieved from https://digiday.com/media/ how-swedish-newspaper-dagens-nyheter-halved-churn-to-8-in-2-years/

Stanca, L., Gui, M., & Gallucci, M. (2013). Attracted but unsatisfied: The effects of sensational content on television consumption choices. *Journal of Media Economics, 26*(2), 82–97. https://doi.org/10.1080/08997764.2013.785552

Stone L. (n.d.). *Continuous partial attention*. Retrieved from https://lindastone.net/ qa/continuous-partial-attention/

Stromback, J., Djerf-Pierre, M., & Shehata, A. (2012). The dynamics of political interest and news media consumption: A longitudinal perspective. *International Journal of Public Opinion Research, 25*(4), 414–435. https://doi.org/10.1093/ijpor/eds018

Swart, J., Peters, C., & Broersma, M. (2018). Shedding light on the dark social: The connective role of news and journalism in social media communities. *New Media & Society, 20*(11), 4329–4345. https://doi.org/10.1177/1461444818772063

Syvertsen, T. (2017). *Media resistance. Protest, dislike, abstention.* New York: Palgrave Macmillan.

Syvertsen, T., & Enli, G. (2019). Digital detox: Media resistance and the promise of authenticity. *Convergence: The International Journal of Research into New Media Technologies,* 1–15. https://doi.org/10.1177/1354856519847325

Tandoc, E. C., Jr. (2014). Journalism is twerking? How web analytics is changing the process of gatekeeping. *New Media & Society, 16*(4), 559–575. https://doi.org/10.1177/1461444814530541

Tandoc, E. C. Jr. (2019). *Analyzing analytics: Disrupting journalism one click at a time.* Oxford: Routledge.

Tandoc, E. C. Jr., Ling, R., Westlund, O., Duffy, A., Goh, D., & Zheng Wei, L. (2018). Audiences' acts of authentication in the age of fake news: A conceptual framework. *New Media & Society, 20*(8), 2745–2763. https://doi.org/10.1177/1461444817731756

Tandoc, E. C., Jr., & Thomas, R. J. (2015). The ethics of web analytics. *Digital Journalism, 3*(2), 243–258. https://doi.org/10.1080/21670811.2014.909122

Tenenboim, O., & Cohen, A. A. (2015). What prompts users to click and comment: A longitudinal study of online news. *Journalism: Theory, Practice & Criticism, 16*(2), 198–217. https://doi.org/10.1177/1464884913513996

Tewksbury, D. (2003). What do Americans really want to know? Tracking the behavior of news readers on the internet. *Journal of Communication, 53*(4), 694–710. https://doi.org/10.1111/j.1460-2466.2003.tb02918.x

Thrift, N. (2008). *Non-representational theory: Space, politics, affect.* London: Routledge.

Throop, C. J. (2003). Articulating experience. *Anthropological Theory, 3*(2), 219–241. https://doi.org/10.1177/1463499603003002006

Thurman, N. (2018). Newspaper consumption in the mobile age. *Journalism Studies, 19*(10), 1409–1429. https://doi.org/10.1080/1461670x.2017.1279028

Thurman, N., & Fletcher, R. (2018). Are Newspapers Heading Toward Post-Print Obscurity? *Digital Journalism, 6*(8), 1003–1017. https://doi.org/10.1080/21670811.2018.1504625

Thurman, N., & Fletcher, R. (2019). Has digital distribution rejuvenated readership? *Journalism Studies, 20*(4), 542–562. https://doi.org/10.1080/14616870x.2017.1397532

Toff, B., & Nielsen, R. K. (2018). "I just google it": Folk theories of distributed discovery. *Journal of Communication, 68*(3), 636–657. https://doi.org/10.1093/joc/jqy009

Toff, B., & Palmer, R. A. (2019). Explaining the Gender Gap in News Avoidance: "News-Is-for-Men" Perceptions and the Burdens of Caretaking. *Journalism Studies, 20*(11), 1563–1579. https://doi.org/10.1080/1461670x.2018.1528882

Tracy, S. J. (2010). Qualitative quality: Eight "big-tent" criteria for excellent qualitative research. *Qualitative Inquiry*, *16*(10), 837–851. https://doi.org/10.1177/1077800410383121

Tsfati, Y., & Cappella, J. N. (2003). Do people watch what they do not trust? *Communication Research*, *30*(5), 504–529. https://doi.org/10.1177/0093650203253371

Tuan, Y. F. (1977). *Space and place: The perspective of experience*. Minneapolis: University of Minnesota Press.

Tversky, A., & Kahneman, D. (1983). Extensional versus intuitive reasoning: The conjunction fallacy in probability judgment. *Psychological Review*, *90*(4), 293–315. https://doi.org/10.1037/0033-295x.90.4.293

Usher, N. (2013). Al Jazeera English online. *Digital Journalism*, *1*(3), 335–351. https://doi.org/10.1080/21670811.2013.801690

Van Damme, K. (2020). Transforming journalism, transforming audiences? Audience-centred research on news use in the omnipresent news environment (PhD thesis). Universiteit Gent, Gent.

Van Damme, K., Courtois, C., Verbrugge, K., & De Marez, L. (2015). What's APPening to news? A mixed-method audience-centred study on mobile news consumption. *Mobile Media & Communication*, *3*(2), 196–213. https://doi.org/10.1177/2050157914557691

Van den Bulck, J. (2006). Television News Avoidance: Exploratory Results From a One-Year Follow-Up Study. *Journal of Broadcasting & Electronic Media*, *50*(2), 231–252. https://doi.org/10.1207/s15506878jobem5002_4

van den Haak, M., De Jong, M., & Jan Schellens, P. (2003). Retrospective vs. concurrent think-aloud protocols: Testing the usability of an online library catalogue. *Behaviour & Information Technology*, *22*(5), 339–351. https://doi.org/10.1080/0044929031000

van der Wurff, R., & Schönbach, K. (2014). Audience expectations of media accountability in the Netherlands. *Journalism Studies*, *15*(2), 121–137. https://doi.org/10.1080/1461670x.2013.801679

van Dijck, J. (2013). "You have one identity": Performing the self on Facebook and LinkedIn. *Media, Culture & Society*, *35*(2), 199–215. https://doi.org/10.1177/0163443712468605

van Dijck, J., & Poell, T. (2013). Understanding Social Media Logic. *Media and Communication*, *1*(1), 2-14.

Verbeek, P. P. (2005). *What things do: Philosophical relations on technology, agency, and design*. University Park: Pennsylvania State University Press.

von Krogh, T., & Andersson, U. (2016). Reading patterns in print and online newspapers. *Digital Journalism*, *4*(8), 1058–1072. https://doi.org/10.1080/21670811.2015.1111158

Vu, H. T. (2014). The online audience as gatekeeper: The influence of reader metrics on news editorial selection. *Journalism: Theory, Practice & Criticism*, *15*(8), 1094–1110. https://doi.org/10.1177/1464884913504259

Wagner, M. C., & Boczkowski, P. J. (2019). The reception of fake news: The interpretations and practices that shape the consumption of perceived misinformation. *Digital Journalism*, *7*(7), 870–885. https://doi.org/10.1080/21670811.2019.1653208

Wahl-Jorgensen, K. (2009). On the newsroom-centricity of journalism ethnography. In S. E. Bird (Ed.), *Journalism and anthropology* (pp. 21–35). Bloomington: Indiana University Press.

Waterson, J. (2020, April 29). Guardian reports surge in readers' support over past year. *Theguardian.com*. Retrieved from www.theguardian.com/media/2020/apr/29/guardian-reports-surge-in-readers-support-over-past-year

Webster, J. G. (2014). *The marketplace of attention: How audiences take shape in a digital age*. Cambridge, MA: MIT Press.

Welbers, K., van Atteveldt, W., Kleinnijenhuis, J., Ruigrok, N., & Schaper, J. (2016). News selection criteria in the digital age: Professional norms versus online audience metrics. *Journalism: Theory, Practice & Criticism*, *17*(8), 1037–1053. https://doi.org/10.1177/1464884915595474

Wennekers, Annemarie, and Jos de Haan. (2017). Nederlanders en nieuws: Gebruik van nieuwsmedia via oude en nieuwe kanalen. *Sociaal en Cultuur Planbureau*. Retrieved from www.scp.nl/Publicaties/Alle_publicaties/Publicaties_2017/Nederlanders_en_nieuws

Wertz, F. J., Charmaz, K., McMullen, M., Josselson, R., Anderson, R., & McSpadden, E. (2011). *Five ways of doing qualitative analysis phenomenological psychology, grounded theory, discourse analysis, narrative research, and intuitive inquiry*. New York: Guilford Press.

Wetherell, M., Taylor, S., & Yates, S. J. (Eds.) (2001). *Discourse Theory and Practice: A Reader*. London: Sage.

Wieland, M., & Kleinen-von Königslöw, K. (2020). Conceptualizing different forms of news processing following incidental news contact: A triple-path model. *Journalism*, 1–18. https://doi.org/10.1177/1464884920915353

Woodstock, L. (2014). The news-democracy narrative and the unexpected benefits of limited news consumption: The case of news resisters. *Journalism: Theory, Practice & Criticism*, *15*(7), 834–849. https://doi.org/10.1177/1464884913504260

Ytre-Arne, B. (2011). "I want to hold it in my hands": Readers' experiences of the phenomenological differences between women's magazines online and in print. *Media, Culture & Society*, *33*(3), 467–477. https://doi.org/10.1177/0163443711398766

Ytre-Arne, B., & Moe, H. (2018). Approximately informed, occasionally monitorial? Reconsidering normative citizen ideals. *International Journal of Press/Politics*, *23*(2), 227–246. https://doi.org/10.1177/1940161218771903

Zamith, R. (2018). Quantified audiences in news production. *Digital Journalism*, *6*(4), 418–435. https://doi.org/10.1080/21670811.2018.1444999

Zelizer, B. (2018). Epilogue: Timing the study of news temporality. *Journalism: Theory, Practice & Criticism*, *19*(1), 111–121. https://doi.org/10.1177/1464884916688964

Zerba, A. (2011). Young adults' reasons behind avoidances of daily print newspapers and their ideas for change. *Journalism & Mass Communication Quarterly*, *88*(3), 597–614. https://doi.org/10.1177/107769901108800308

Zillmann, D. (1988). Mood management through communication choices. *American Behavioral Scientist*, *31*(3), 327–340. https://doi.org/10.1177/000276488031003005

Zumpolle, C. (2017). *"De één houdt van zoet en de ander houdt van drop." Een kwalitatief onderzoek naar overwegingen en factoren die een rol spelen bij news avoidance. ["One likes sweet and the other likes liquorice." A qualitative study of considerations and factors that play a role in news avoidance]* (MA-thesis). Vrije Universiteit Amsterdam, Amsterdam.

Appendix
Overview of incorporated research projects 2004–2020

Table A.1 Overview of incorporated research projects 2004–2020

Research project	Audience/users	Scale
2004–2005 – How NOS News can accommodate a younger audience (15–25)	96 in-depth interviews, 143 short interviews with young people, 45 news biographies, 65 online open questionnaires, 37 mood boards, and 43 interviews with journalism students, 100 street interviews (aged 15–85)	National
2009–2011 – Participatory journalism: the impact of neighborhood journalism (Research assistants and interviewers: Jolien Arendsen, Mariska van der Sluis, Mark Merks, Eva van Mossevelde, Marloes van Diffelen, Diana Kreemers) (Interviewers: Annemieke Boogert, Daniel Nokes, Diewertje Kuiper, Ilona de Jong, Irene van Wijhe, Ischa Klaassen, Kim Schoot, Lenneke Arts, Madelon Meester, Marijn de Vries, Marjolein Schurink, Nienke Vos, Reina Louw, Roel Rutjens, Saskia van Gils, Tessy Nelissen, Tineke van der Zwaag)	33 in-depth interviews and 24 intercept-interviews	Local and hyper-local

(Continued)

Table A.1 (Continued)

Research project	Audience/users	Scale
2011 – The news demands and news habits of (young) iPad and smartphone users (Interviewer: Madelon Meester)	14 in-depth interviews (including think-aloud protocol, visual cues)	National
2012 – The news habits and viewing experiences of young (25–35) and old (55–65) (Interviewer: Tim Groot Kormelink)	12 in-depth interviews (including think-aloud protocol, audiovisual cues, ranking exercises)	National
2012–2013 – Tailor-made news: meeting the demands of news users on mobile and social media (Interviewer: Tim Groot Kormelink)	24 in-depth interviews (including sensory ethnography, think-aloud protocol, ranking exercises), survey ($N = 270$)	National
2012–2013 – The value of transparency (Interviewer: Martje Doeve)	19 in-depth interviews (including sensory ethnography, think-aloud protocol, ranking exercises), survey ($N = 263$)	National
2014 – The motives, experiences, and considerations of news users when clicking and browsing online news (Interviewers: Marrit van den Akker, Chris Pruissen, Stacey Bovet, Diana Koning, Janine Renes, Karel van Hasselt, Steven Wiltjer)	56 in-depth interviews with younger (20–35) and older (50–65) online news users (including think-aloud protocol)	National
2015 – When viewers experience political information as captivating (Interviewers: Leonie Durlinger, Inger van Tuinen, Neeltje de Quaij, Jennifer Groeneveld, Rutger Westerhof, Arther van Ree, Stefan Heijdra, Steffan Konings, Sander Grégoire)	54 in-depth interviews (including watching and discussing video clips)	National
2014 - What is important and interesting in the region? (Project leader: Irene Costera Meijer; researchers: Hildebrand Bijleveld, Marrit Van den Akker, Chris Pruissen, Steven Wiltjer, Ferdy Hazeleger)	132 intercept interviews (10–15 minutes) 10 focus group interviews (2.5 hours) Online survey (416 people) via websites of public regional broadcasters, Facebook, and Twitter 15 in-depth interviews with regional stakeholders 7 in-depth interviews with representatives of local media	Regional, local

Research project	Audience/users	Scale
2016 – Capturing material and sensory dimensions of news use (Interviewer: Tim Groot Kormelink)	13 in-depth interviews (two-sided video-ethnography)	National
2017 – Experiencing news avoidance (Interviewers: Caspar Zumpolle, José Honing, Luca Goossens)	24 qualitative street interviews (400 respondents); in-depth interviews with 6 low-frequency users and 6 high-frequency users; 10 in-depth interviews with people who intentionally avoid the news	National
2017 – How users experience climate journalism (Interviewer: Marieke Theunissen)	10 in-depth interviews (25–40 years) (including ranking exercises, day in the life)	National
2017 – Experiencing news enjoyment (Interviewer: Runak Sharaf)	10 in-depth interviews (including ranking exercises, day in the life)	National
2017 – When trust and truth matter (Interviewers: Caspar Zumpolle, Robert Zomers, Runak Sharaf, José Honing, Britt Kenter, Melanie Jong Tjien Fa, Janis Bodzinga, Marieke Theunissen, Luca Goossens, Kristel Struiksma, Samira Ramsahai, Guus Daamen, Deborah van Harten, Anne Lotte Hendriks, Eline Dijkstra, Didier Jansen, Jens Bezemer, Bob Vek, Loes van Langen, Sanae Samhi, Kees Gort, Dennis van Diest, Sylvana van den Braak, Frank Breukelman, Suzanne Rijnja)	75 in-depth interviews (including ranking exercises)	National
2018 – When trust and truth matter (Interviewers: Rowan Koeleman, Tessa Assen, Julia Dijkers, Myrthe Gils, Sarah Haddou, Marie-Louise Hoogendoorn, Kurt Kooiman, Merel Kuipers, Suzanne Rijnja, Freek Schröder, Bart Nietveld, Lisanne Zwaneveld, Mike Megens, Celine Sulsters, Jana Flekken)	33 in-depth interviews (including ranking exercises)	National

(*Continued*)

Table A.1 (Continued)

Research project	Audience/users	Scale
2018 – How Dutch Muslims experience the media representation of Islam and Muslims (Interviewer: Sarah Haddou)	11 in-depth interviews with Muslims also having participated in the media	National
2018 – How extreme right-wing voters experience news (Interviewer: Suzanne Rijnja)	10 in-depth interviews with creative methods	National
2019 – How users experience news about Black Pete (Interviewer: Celine Sulsters)	12 in-depth interviews (black and white informants)	National
2019 – How teens experience news on Instagram (Interviewer: Rachel Stoffelsen)	10 in-depth interviews	National
2019 – How users experience a Facebook detox (Interviewers: Rowan Koeleman, Rachel Stoffelsen)	12 in-depth interviews (following a one-week Facebook detox)	National
2019–2020 – News habit formation: how people (start) to develop a new habit (Interviewers: Tim Groot Kormelink, Devran Alkaş, Lisa Kiewiet, Frédérique Blaauw, Doortje Linssen, Elisabetta Santangalo, Anne Klein Gunnewiek, Catherine Kleynen, Laura Otto, Brendan Hadden, Niels van den Berg, Fay Degenkamp, Sanne Harmes, Tosia Hogema, Madelief Krikken, Rosalie Overing, Noor van Pelt, Murielle Posthuma, Pepijn Keppel, Joost Schutte, Floris Spaans, Bart Timmer, Tibbe Dolman)	80 in-depth interviews (following a three-week newspaper trial subscription)	National
2020 – Everyday news podcast use (Interviewers: Lisa Kiewiet, Frédérique Blaauw, Doortje Linssen, Elisabetta Santangelo, Brendan Hadden)	60 in-depth interviews	National

Index

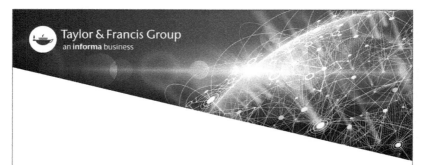